(Christmas 1989)

STRE

~~please read it!!~~

D0484628

BARTER BOOKS
SEAHOUSES
NORTHUMBERLAND

SANTA MONICA
SEAHORSE
WORTHING W. S.

Streetwise

JOHN GOODFELLOW

WITH ANDY BUTCHER

YOUTH WITH A MISSION
AMSTERDAM
KINGSWAY PUBLICATIONS
EASTBOURNE

Copyright © John Goodfellow and Andrew Butcher 1989

First published 1989

All rights reserved.
No part of this publication may be reproduced or
transmitted in any form or by any means, electronic
or mechanical, including photocopy, recording, or any
information storage and retrieval system, without
permission in writing from the publisher.

Front cover design by Vic Mitchell

British Library Cataloguing in Publication Data

Goodfellow, John
    Streetwise.
    1. Christian life. Personal observations
    I. Title   II. Butcher, Andy
    248.4

    ISBN 0–86065–735–3

Youth With a Mission (YWAM) is an international
movement of Christians from many denominations, united in Christ
and dedicated to presenting him personally to this generation.
Youth With a Mission 13 Highfield Oval, Ambrose Lane,
Harpenden, Herts AL5 4BX (Tel 0582 65481)
and at Kadijksplein 18, 1018 AC, Amsterdam,
(Tel 010–31–20–279536)

Printed in Great Britain for
KINGSWAY PUBLICATIONS LTD
Lottbridge Drove, Eastbourne, E Sussex BN23 6NT by
Richard Clay Ltd, Bungay, Suffolk

To Floyd and Sally McClung

– for your love, friendship and humble walk with God

Contents

Acknowledgements

This book wouldn't have been written without the prayers, practical help and support of some very dear people.

First, I want to thank my wife, Terry, for helping me find the time to work on the manuscript, and providing the fine detail my memory missed. I'm grateful, too, for Mandy Butcher's patience in freeing her husband, Andy, to spend so many evenings at the typewriter putting our conversations together. Andy took this on despite his already heavy work load as Editor of Christian Family magazine at that time.

My sister, Trish, brother-in-law, Jamie, and Mum provided timely encouragement and comment as the project developed. Sister Joan helped in this way, too, as well as typing some of the manuscript along with Myrtle Thompson.

Finally, I'm indebted to Floyd McClung for his initial spur to put pen to paper, in the hope and belief that telling this story may be a way that God will touch and change other people's lives in the way he has mine.

I have changed the actual names of a few of the people and places where it seemed appropriate to do so. But most are identified, and all the incidents and experiences are recounted just as I remember they happened.

John Goodfellow

Introduction

Owning Up

I pulled the cast-iron gate closed behind me, and as it snapped shut I paused for a moment with my hand resting on the cold metal. 'It could well be bars of a different kind by tonight, John,' I thought to myself as I flicked the gate rods, taking a last look up at the house. Would I be coming back?

The prospect of this being a one-way journey brought my senses alive as I strolled up the quiet street in the cool, spring morning air. I looked around at the other houses – tall, well-decorated semis – as I passed by. How welcoming and warm they looked, with their bright front doors and stylish curtains. What a pleasant area this was to live in ... how could its calm, peaceful pleasantness have escaped me for so long?

Up round the corner I crossed the main road, busy with traffic heading for the city centre and another week's commuting and cursing the queues. My first appointment was over on the other side, a couple of hundred yards away. The muscles in my stomach started to tighten, and as the building loomed closer my steps slowed slightly.

Pictures of just what I could well be letting myself in for flashed across my mind, chased hard by the idea that I could simply crumple up the list I was fingering in my pocket, throw it away and forget all about this crazy business.

No one would ever know, after all. I could drop the screwed-up paper into the gutter, and it would soon be swept up with all the empty cigarette packets and fish-and-chip wrappers. Out of sight, out of mind. Just another scrap of litter on the municipal dump. Maybe a seagull would even carry it off somewhere remote.

But I knew that it wasn't really that easy. The refuse collectors may cart off the words I had scribbled there, but nothing could remove what they stood for. I had to complete the task on which I had set out. Straightening my tie again nervously, I took one last deep breath and pushed open the door. This was it.

It was just a few minutes after opening, so I didn't have to wait long before I was greeted by one of the clerks at the enquiries counter. She flashed me one of her best Monday morning smiles.

'Hello, sir, can I help you?'

'Good morning. Yes, please. I'd like to see the manager if that's at all possible.'

'Certainly. Could you tell me what it is in connection with, please?'

That threw me for a moment. I had a vague idea of what I intended to say, but I'd not expected to start quite yet. I hesitated. 'Well, it's very confidential and important. It needn't take very long....'

She looked at me quizzically for a moment or two. Despite my best efforts, it was all too obvious that I wasn't used to living in a suit and collar. With my long hair and beard I hardly fitted the bill of the average businessman, and she seemed to notice that the tie felt as though it was tightening like a noose round the growing lump in my throat. She slipped away to an office at the rear.

The seconds stretched into long minutes, and I had to fight the urge that was rising in me to turn round and walk quickly out. It still wasn't too late to forget this crazy business! And then she was back, and with another smile she was opening the security door and leading me through into the manager's office, beyond the brass plaque and solid oak door.

Half-rising from behind his broad, dark wooden desk, he greets me with a smile that is checked by his obvious uncertainty as to quite what I want an appointment for. But he recovers his executive composure swiftly, and with a sweep of his right hand invites me to take the seat in front of him, set slightly at an angle.

The moment is here, the thing I've known has to be done. And despite the confidence I have that it is right, apprehension grips me. Only the anchor of my break-fast prevents my stomach from doing a double flip and leaping out of my mouth. Galvanised by anxiety, I don't even wait until he's seated again.

I stretch out my right hand to shake his, and launch into my half-rehearsed speech.

'Good morning' – accompanied by my best effort at a confident smile. 'Thank you for agreeing to see me. My name is John Goodfellow . . .' and as the words start to flow it's like a button has been pressed deep inside. A warm sense of security seems to flood my body. This is right, it's OK – everything is going to work out.

'. . . and I don't know if you remember me or not, but I was a customer of yours for several years.'

He looks at me encouragingly but without recognition. Fingers stroke the side of his blotting pad – green, clean and just changed for the coming week, no doubt – as he waits for me to continue.

'And, well, I want you to know that I have recently become a Christian, and I feel that God has told me to come to you today and to confess to the fact that I owe you a lot of money.'

His face registers confusion for a moment, and I press on to spare him having to try to respond.

'When I had an account here, I cashed many cheques with no way of meeting them from my balance, and then ignored all your letters demanding repayment. I did it intentionally and deliberately, with no thought of repay-ing you. I stole it all, in effect. I'm very sorry about that now, and I would like to ask your forgiveness for doing it, sir.'

He nods slowly and silently, with a continuing look of puzzlement, as I go on. 'And I would like to pay back all the money that I owe you. I hope to be starting work very soon, and will be able to post the first instalment to you in a fortnight or so, if that is all right?'

By now he seems more nervous than I was when I entered the bank a few minutes earlier. He laces his fingers together on the desktop and responds as though we have simply just completed an ordinary business transaction.

'Well, thank you,' as he takes my name and address, 'that all seems to be in order. Fine. We appreciate your having come in like this, and I look forward to receiving your first payment before the end of the month. Thank you.'

And within minutes I'm out on the street again, sucking in the fresh air with relief and gratitude. With rising confidence I step out across the road and on to the next address on the list.

By the end of the day I'd walked and talked myself bone tired. The feelings of nervousness before each appointment hadn't entirely gone, but they had decreased with each visit. It was a tremendous feeling to push open the front gate again – I patted it 'hello' as I came through – and walk up the path.

Since leaving home that morning, I'd visited half a dozen locations around the town and admitted that I had been a thief, a common criminal. I had explained how I had taken their money and property – in some cases without them ever having discovered the loss. I told them that I was sorry, and that I wanted to pay back every penny.

And I gave them the opportunity to call the police, if that was what they wanted to do – even though I was already due to appear in court to face another criminal charge, and knew that the reporting of any further offences would almost certainly ensure that I went to prison for a long time.

I'd been prepared to go down. The idea frightened me a little – my mouth had gone dry a couple of times as I explained the purpose of my unannounced visit, and waited to see if their hand would reach for the telephone. It had been a distinct possibility when I set out that morning. Back home, I was thrilled to have made my peace and been spared what could have been the harsh consequences.

But what burned even more brightly within me was the excitement of having been able to explain to a couple of those I had visited just what had made me set out on such an apparently risky and unnecessary venture.

It was the story of someone desperately trying to put together the pieces of a broken life. But for him it was like trying to complete an abstract jigsaw puzzle with no master pattern to follow. And as each piece in turn failed to fit, there grew an increasing sense of anger, frustration and despair.

Sex, drink, drugs, violence, crime, occultism; they had all tumbled together in a meaningless jumble. Until just when it seemed too late, just when there seemed to be no hope of making any sense of it all, he'd found the way to put the pieces in their right place.

He was me, and I had met Jesus Christ.

That list of addresses in my jacket pocket symbolised the first half of a life that had contained no hope and little meaning. With the new purpose I possessed, I was excited at what could be written on a clean sheet.

1

Street Fighting Man

The beer was free, and you didn't need to pay more than a half-hearted compliment to get one of the young holidaymaking girls to spend the night with you.

Working in a bar on Spain's tourist coast was everything I'd been promised and hoped for; an endless round of drink and free sex that somehow only made you thirst for more. And if the pace of fast living ever got a bit too much, there was always a plentiful supply of drugs to charge you up for another night of partying.

By daylight you would probably have just dismissed the Crazy Horse Saloon as a shabby, hastily-constructed set of a second-rate cowboy film. Thrown together in rough cheap wood, with a large verandah facing the dusty street, it seemed a little out of place only a couple of hundred yards from the beach at Santa Suzanna, a small seaside town just outside Lorette del Mar.

But by night it took on an altogether brighter image, putting on its best face for the public. It turned into one of the top nightspots for the young sunseekers who were flooding into Spain with the package holiday boom. Nightly, scores of young people from England, Holland and Germany crowded into the cavernous bar, where they would drink noisily and dance until 2 am – and later.

For a small-time crook with a drink problem and a growing dislike for the hard graft of bricklaying in the wet, cold British Midlands, it was like paradise. I had been delighted when two friends who had been contracted to run the place for the summer season asked me to join the bar staff. The fact that our drinks were on the house, for as long as we could stand on our feet, was an added bonus.

For some strange reason, the visiting girls were impressed by our macho image. They had come from their boring nine-to-five jobs in anonymous offices in grey cities, looking for a holiday romance. We were as close as they got. At the end of each night there would always be a group of them waiting behind – giggling, and slightly the worse for wear – for us to choose from. We'd pair off dispassionately and decide which couples would get to go back to the staff quarters – a cramped, dirty bunkhouse at the rear of the bar – and who would go back to the girls' hotels, where we would give the nightwatchmen a knowing leer as we crept past.

Most mornings I would wake up wondering first where I was, then who I was with, and finally where I could find a drink to get rid of the awful throb in my head. If we never even exchanged names, then it was all right by me; I didn't particularly want to see her again, and some of her friends would probably be in line the next night. Once the night's passion was spent, I couldn't wait for them to get their clothes on and go.

Then I'd stumble out of bed about mid-day, and meet up with the other lads for a large cooked breakfast, washed down by a few pints of beer to get the circulation going again. We'd swap stories and comments about the girls, comparing notes like buyers at a cattle market. Then it would be time to catch up on some sleep in the sun for an hour or so before heading off on our daily 'propaganda patrol'. We'd strut along the beach like we owned the place, handing out leaflets and urging all the sunbathers to come along to the Crazy Horse Saloon that evening.

Not that we worked hard for the sake of it. The more customers that were there, the more opportunity there was to rip them off or get them into bed – or both. It was as simple as that. We would be keen to see everyone spend as much as possible, so we'd whip up the party atmosphere, joining in the dancing and larking with the customers, generally behaving as though we were having a great time. But there would always be one eye out for the chance to carve an unwary girl away from her circle of friends, or to steal.

One of the simplest ways we found to make money on the side was to shortchange someone. As it started to get late, people drank more and the place became even more sweaty and crowded, so it was easy to delay returning with someone's change for a while. I'd keep half an eye on them and if they persisted I'd go and make a vague excuse about having been kept busy and then try to shortchange them, hoping they didn't notice. More often than not they didn't, and the secret pocket I'd made in my uniform would be bulging with stolen notes by closing time.

In an atmosphere charged with alcohol and sex, violence was never far away. We welcomed it with open arms and clenched fists as the only thing missing to make our job satisfaction complete. Partly we recognised that if we could win a reputation as the toughest team of bouncers on the coast, then we would have less trouble to cope with; and partly because we knew how it impressed some of the girls, and a little bit because we simply revelled in a good fight. So we dealt with any problems ruthlessly and efficiently.

If someone started to create a scene – maybe over a girl, a spilled drink or an unguarded remark – they would be bundled outside unceremoniously and given a swift beating, before being advised to get on their way. As far as we were concerned, the cardinal sin a customer could commit was to hit a fellow waiter. It happened from time to time if one of us was a little too slow in sorting out a situation, or if we were caught trying to get away with someone's change. But within seconds the assailant would be felled by two or three other bouncers.

Outside he'd be held down and kicked and stamped on viciously. We broke arms, legs and ribs – and laughed as the victims crawled away. As long as we didn't disturb the locals, the Spanish police didn't really care too much what happened to some unfortunate holidaymaker who'd had a bit too much to drink and maybe fallen on their way home.

We weren't too keen on allowing Spanish visitors into the saloon because they weren't as freespending as the well-heeled holidaymakers, and simply blocked the bar space, slowing down trade. We also had some complaints that the Spanish men were pestering the girls; claims that brought out a muddled sort of patriotic gallantry. So we tried generally to discourage them from staying too long – until one night.

It was getting on for closing, and most people had already drifted away. The floor was awash with spilled beer, empty glasses and cigarette packets, as usual. The air was thick with tobacco and the smell of cheap perfume. We were trying to clear up so that we could get away to meet the latest groups of girls, but a small group of local men insisted on being served with one last drink. They wouldn't take no for an answer, and then one of them reached out and swung an ashtray round, crashing it over Dave's head.

That was it. The place exploded in a flurry of kicks, punches and oaths. They were outnumbered, but the leader was a big bull of a man – he looked as though he had escaped from one of the local arenas. It took four of us to subdue him as his friends fled. Finally we battered him to the ground, and dragged him outside where we laid into him with our fists and boots. We left him in the dust, moaning quietly. When he fell silent, I thought that we might have killed him.

Satisfied that he was still alive, we spat on him and turned back inside. The thrill of combat led to more celebratory drinks all round, and inflated our view of ourselves as the meanest, toughest crew around. We enjoyed our notoriety, and were greatly pleased at the way customers held us in awe as the story of the fight was subsequently embellished and retold.

A couple of weeks later word filtered back through the grapevine that our victim had been badly hurt. He was a popular figure in the area, and had ended up in hospital with severe internal injuries, a broken arm, fractured leg and cracked ribs. The rumour was that a revenge attack was planned.

We took this threat seriously. In our off-duty moments we fashioned ourselves a brutal armoury to repel any would-be attackers. There were iron bars, wooden clubs with nails driven through or wrapped with barbed wire, bottles and bricks. I selected a three-foot long wooden stave and painstakingly carved jagged teeth into the end. When we had all finished, we posed for a photograph, trying to outboast each other as to what we'd do if called on to use our weapons. Wearing building site hardhats and clutching our batons and bars, we lined up for the photographer with big grins, in a crude parody of a victorious football team.

For a week or so we were especially careful to be on our guard, and meticulous about checking every visitor to the Crazy Horse Saloon. But then the free drink and rich pickings must have made us careless. One night I was grabbed by the arm by one of the other waiters as I passed from the bar with a trayful of orders.

'Johnny, look over there in the corner,' he shouted in my ear, above the drumming disco beat.

'Where?' I turned and looked where he was pointing. Over in the corner, in one of the darker parts of the room, away from the dancefloor, were a couple of faces that seemed familiar from that earlier night. We both scanned the room more closely, and to our horror spotted two or three other young men who had been involved in the fight.

A hurried council of war was held at the bar, and we decided that we had better close early. Some excuse was offered by the DJ, and we managed to usher everyone out apologetically. Then we locked and bolted the doors, and gathered together at the shuttered windows. A small group of men could be seen standing just at the end of the street. Wolf cries and shouts carried as we reached behind the bar for our weapons.

All went quiet for a few minutes, and then they were at the door. They must have been using a log or a bench as a battering ram, because they pounded their way in through the heavy doors. As soon as they burst through we set upon them, and a bloody brawl ensued in the darkened bar. Chairs were thrown and sticks swung. We managed to beat them back and then, suddenly, they bolted.

Inflamed by the fighting, we whooped and ran out after them into the street. As we turned the corner in pursuit we realised what a dreadful mistake we had made. There were another fifteen or so heavily-armed men – batons, bricks and bars – making more than thirty in all. The others stepped in behind, blocking our escape. The twelve of us had run straight into a trap.

Fear and hatred swirl together to fuel my arms as I swing them wildly around my head, lashing out with my stave in all directions. Everywhere around me in the grey moonlight is a blur of bodies, a fog of violence. Screams of pain and shouts of fury mix with the sickening thud of wood and metal on flesh and bone. Grunts and sighs follow the impact.

The sheer weight of numbers presses us back, and in a moment of rational thought plucked somehow from the storm of the fighting I realise: 'If one of us goes down, we'll never get up again. They aim to kill us!' My blood runs cold.

A thick-set, curly-haired man with an iron bar lunges forward, trying to smash it across my head. I manage to jerk to one side, ducking his blow, and swing my heavy rod savagely, clenching my teeth to throw every ounce of aggression into the movement. It connects, shattering his cheekbone, and jarring my hands painfully. I give out a satisfied yell before stepping forward, pulling my stave back ready for another strike. 'Come on, which one of you is next!'

The fear has gone. In its place is an ordered, calm appreciation of how pleasing it is to inflict serious injury. I face the next man stepping into my path and try to decide where to hit him for the maximum damage, with grim enjoyment.

It's still and quiet all of a sudden, but for the gasping for breath and raw terror all around. We face the other gang, a few yards away, and are sharing a common thought – the fighting seems to have transformed us into a machine of violence. 'It's no use us trying to run for it: we'll never make it. ...'

By now the smell of violence has intoxicated me so much that it seems to have triggered off my last safety valve. 'OK, then, let's go and get the dirty ...' and with a roar I spring forward, leading a charge at the surprised enemy.

Pain bursts across my face in a rainbow of sensations, and there's something warm on my cheek. Blood. A hurled brick splits open the skin, down to the bone, as broken bottles, chains, bars and other weapons are wielded again.

Triumph fills me as I see them start to break and run. It takes a few moments to realise that it's not us they're fleeing from. Residents terrified by the vicious battle boiling over in the street below their windows have called the police. La Garda has arrived in force.

I drop my stick to the ground and touch the wound on the side of my face gently. The fighting is over, and all I can think is how I wish I'd had the chance to smash someone else real good before it ended.

Not surprisingly, we weren't exactly popular with the Spanish authorities. But the locals with whom we had been tangling hadn't wanted to hang around to explain what was going on, so we poured out a story of how we had been defending ourselves from an attempted armed robbery.

I don't think they really believed us for one moment, but there were no other witnesses to the fighting's early moments. So they had no choice but to believe our tale and leave the matter there.

Pretty soon any vague memories of having been scared or horrified by the brutality had been washed away in a few rounds of celebratory drinks, and our reputation grew. For the next few weeks we were even granted a police guard to make sure that there were no further 'attempted robberies'.

Thankfully, the policemen who were keeping a protective eye on us didn't step inside, though. Had they done so, what little tolerance they had left for us would have evaporated instantly. The Spanish authorities were ruthless in opposing the spread of drugs – there were harsh penalties for people found possessing or pushing. But that didn't stop us from risking arrest.

Even just a few weeks of living with my foot hard down on the accelerator had swept away any last grains of self-control or restraint that I may have possessed within me. I soon found myself using drugs heavily, despite having sworn to myself that I would never touch them again after a frightening first-time experience.

It had happened the previous year – again in Spain, on my first working trip for the summer season. It had turned out to be fairly unsuccessful, because by the time I arrived all the good jobs in the bars and discos had already gone. I managed to find temporary work in a small drinking place in Lorette del Mar, but it was well off the beaten track and I soon got bored. It had none of the action I'd been promised. To pass the time after closing, one night, I went along to the disco-bar popular with all the other English seasonal workers.

There, over a couple of beers, I was offered a tab of

LSD – 'acid' – and being a little curious, and a lot concerned that I shouldn't seem chicken, I'd swallowed it down. But as the psychedelic drug bubbled through my bloodstream, I was pitched into a frightening trip.

Sitting at a corner table, trying to keep a grip on my rebelling senses, I glanced around and had to rub my eyes hard. It was no good; they were still there. As I gazed around, all the other people – dancing, drinking, talking, laughing – had pigs' heads. It was like something out of a bizarre, comic opera and I laughed aloud to myself, oblivious to the way people looked at me with concern. This was amazing! But it was like being on a rollercoaster, where after every plunge you were slowly and surely winched up for what you knew would be another shock. Yet there was no way to stop it all happening. You just had to sit there and hope that, somehow, you would come through.

The walls started to blister and ripple, seeming to expand and contract in time with my breathing. Colours began to dance in front of my eyes; beautiful globules of rich reds, yellows, blues and greens, twisting and melting into one another in front of me like a giant paint palette. Then I saw that some of the people around me were surrounded with some sort of a strange glow that pulsated in time to the beat of the music. It was like watching colours breathe, with the shades rising and falling in time with my own inhaling and exhaling. As the night wore on, my mind and imagination continued to turn loops and spirals, and I was thankful when the sensations of sight, sound and smell began to recede; so I could finally collapse into bed.

Next morning those experiences seemed frustratingly close at hand, yet impossible to reach. But while I had emerged unscathed, I was too scared or too cautious to risk another 'trip'. The story my friends had told of their group experience – when they had been horrified to see each other apparently with their heads chopped off, blood gushing from the severed arteries – had been enough to convince me of the hazards of dabbling any more.

Besides, I argued, plenty of drink and the chance of 'pulling' a girl were all that I needed.

That's how it had been until the Crazy Horse Saloon. But by the height of the season, my body was already crying out. An endless round of heavy drinking, not enough sleep, poor diet and promiscuous sex was taking its toll. So one night when we were introduced to 'boogaloo' we thought that it was the answer to all our needs.

Amphetamine, speed, uppers – it had a variety of names, but the same effect. After an hour or so, the first four or five tablets would start to make me buzz. It was as though someone had started up a generator deep inside that began throbbing away, pouring more energy into my system. I felt wildly alive, and would talk away nineteen to the dozen, my words accompanied by rapid action and body movements. The rush of the drug kept me constantly fidgety; on the move. It was uncomfortable to stand still for even a moment without hopping from one leg to the other, and we'd serve and carry drinks at a furious pace.

By about midnight it would be time to drop some more, and these would send us scorching through until 3 am or later, when the final late-drinkers were either guided or carried out. But by then we would most likely be too wide awake and full of energy to consider sleep, so we would go into town and meet up with some other English lads for further drinks sessions. With so much 'boogaloo' inside me I felt like King Kong. It pumped me full of all the confidence I lacked in my sober times, and I thought that I'd found what I required to make my life complete.

Sometimes we would push even our stretched bodies and minds to the absolute limit. We would be so switched on that we didn't stop for two or three days at a stretch – partying, working, more partying and more working.

And even then, finally, it was a question of little more than collapsing on the sand for a couple of hours' sleep during the afternoon before getting up, washing another handful of tablets down with a beer or two, and getting ready for another night at the Crazy Horse Saloon.

By and by, though, the numbers started to trail off, and the temperatures began to cool. It was getting towards the end of the season, and after a final, drunken celebration, the cowboy bar pulled down its shutters for the last time that summer.

In a matter of just a few short months, the paradise I thought I had discovered, had exacted a huge toll. My weight had dropped to just over eight stone. My teeth and gums were sore and yellowing. My hair was lank and falling out, and I was addicted to consuming huge quantities of alcohol and drugs.

The party was over, the girls had gone. And as I packed my bags and returned to Nottingham with no job lined up, and the few pounds I had managed not to squander out of the hundreds I had earned and stolen – I wondered just for a moment if it had all been worth it.

For all the girls I'd been with, all the good times my friends and I had drunk to, I arrived home feeling just as empty as I could always remember.

2

Distant Relatives

I'd known from an early age how it was possible to be in
the middle of something and yet feel on the outside.
That's what home had always been like. Our house was
always the centre of a lot of noise, laughter and high
party spirits – yet even as a small child I seemed to be
isolated from it all. Everything always seemed to be
going on just beyond my grasp, and this inability to
reach out was like a clamp that squeezed me tight inside,
keeping me squashed and distant.

As first-generation settlers in England, my parents
were keen to remember their Irish roots, and most
weekends the house would almost hum with the music
and dancing. Crowds of friends would be invited back
from the local pubs for more drinking, dancing and
remembering 'the old days'. Many tears were shed as the
whisky and beer added a rosey hue to the memories of
what were, in reality, more often than not hard times.
And then the blows would follow as the spirits quickened
fiery temperaments.

Dad had arrived in England as a young man back in
1930. He was a Roman Catholic from Tempo, a small
farming community north of the border, not far from
Enniskillen, where even then the seeds of sectarian
enmity were being sown. Despite his willingness to work
hard and a capacity for tough labour, he was unable to
find regular work. So, like so many of his friends before
him, he looked 'across the water' to where opportunities

for hard physical work were plentiful and, by comparison, well rewarded.

He soon found work digging roads with a pipe-laying company in Kent. Tall, broad and with a talent for playing the fiddle, he quickly became a popular figure among the expatriate groups that would meet most nights of the week to drink to and sing of the beloved homeland they had left behind. It was through one of these Irish nights that Harry Goodfellow, or Paddy as he was more commonly known, came to meet a young lass by the name of Bina.

She was from Macroom, near Cork, south of the border. Also a Catholic, she had shown her strength of character and independence at the tender age of fifteen by running away from home to seek employment in England. As one of eight children, she had experienced a happy childhood, but had decided that she wanted still more out of life. By making contact with an older sister who had already made the crossing, she was able to find work as a private maid in Sevenoaks.

By the time they married, Dad had secured a better job, working for Fremlins brewery in the same town. Settling into their first home – rented rooms – my older brother, Tony, was born within the first year of their new life together.

Joan arrived seven years later and I weighed in at just under seven pounds, three years after that. By that time the Goodfellows had moved on again, to the Midland town of Nottingham. The industrial heartland of Britain was growing healthily, and Dad had decided to relocate the family after being invited to go into business with relatives. They operated a haulage company that transported open-cast coal around the region. It suited his temperament down to the ground, combining hard work with a personal pride in giving value for money and good, reliable service. The business prospered, and soon our home was a comfortable, well-appointed house with its own garden – a far cry from my parents' early days.

Dad was well liked and respected by customers, colleagues and friends alike. He was uncompromising, but also scrupulously fair by his own standards of behaviour. He also prided himself in caring for his family – but his love for a drink with the boys would sometimes leave good intentions unfulfilled. On countless occasions I would hear my mother and father rowing late into the night about the money he wasted on drink and friends. What was a man if he couldn't look after his own mates, he would counter, and they would scream back and forth at each other. Sometimes they would throw more than accusations and insults, and I would hear crockery and ornaments crashing against the wall. I remember kneeling against the bannisters at the top of the stairs, my eyes squeezed tight and my jaw clenched hard in the forlorn hope that I could make it all go away.

When they really set to with each other, their rage seemed to know no limits. Dad was always doing home improvements around the place: he spent many hours putting new panelling in around the stairs. Not long afterwards there was another homecoming row after the pubs had shut, and in uncontrolled anger he systematically put his fist through every piece of board that he had only just finished fitting.

I would lie in bed at night – sometimes awake for what seemed like hours – with dread in my heart. What if she really left him, as I'd heard her threaten? I wished so much that they would stop fighting, but their violent disagreements just seemed to fuel their relationship, and act as a strange kind of cement for the love they had for each other, but just couldn't seem to express more tenderly.

Although Dad endeavoured to care for us all well in practical ways, we never seemed to spend much time together as a family. He would either be working long, hard hours, or he would be drinking with his friends down at one of the local Irish pubs.

So I used to relish the times when he would arrive home in time for a big, cooked tea before slipping his jacket on to stroll off for a few beers. Together with Tony and Joan, I'd clamber up onto the sofa with him and beg him to tell us one of his war stories.

He had been one of the first into the services when war had been declared in September 1939. As a bombardier in the Royal Horse Artillery, he had landed in France with the British Expeditionary Force and shared the belief that Germany's military arrogance would be sorted out very quickly.

Dad would hold us all spellbound as he told how he had been in the thick of the fighting in those early days. The British infantry had been forced back under heavy artillery fire, and soon the crack Panzer tank divisions were pushing through. Dad's unit was ordered to blow up their own guns to prevent them being taken and turned on the British army. Then they were to fall back, after delaying the German advance to allow the others to make their way to the French shores.

During their flight, Dad and his group found themselves caught in a bombardment that had them pinned down in a wood for three nights. They joked about sending one of their number over to a nearby vineyard to bring back some bottles to help pass the time. And when they drew straws in a jokey poll, Dad pulled out the short one. True to character, he then took the bet as a serious pledge – and snaked his way over to the building, despite the risk from shells landing all around. Once there he had to lie low for five hours while another barrage screamed overhead, before returning, grinning with his grape trophies.

'And, you know,' he would always say, pausing in the tale as we looked at each other with wide eyes, ' I believe that the hand of God was on me then. . . .'

This conviction was born out of what he said happened next. Arriving finally at Dunkirk, Dad and his friends found a scene of carnage and chaos. Heavy casualties were being inflicted on the British forces as they were plucked from the beaches by an armada of small boats. Dad and his mates dug themselves into foxholes in the sand as they waited their turn to find a spare seat on one of the craft bobbing up and down as close to shore as they dare come. At last they were given the order to run for one of the boats, and they set off at a dash across the sand.

As they charged into the water, two of his friends made for the nearest boat, shouting for him to follow. There were spaces for eight or nine men on board, and they were first in line. But something deep inside told Dad not to head that way. 'No, not that one lads,' he screamed, grabbing them by the arms and pulling them back. Instead they waded across to their right and another, smaller craft in the distance – and as they did so, a direct hit shattered the other boat and the men on board.

Arriving back in Ramsgate on a small liner called The Daffodil, Dad was allowed home leave like many of the other fortunate Dunkirk survivors. And when he returned for further service, he had another experience that convinced him that there was some divine intervention in his military service.

He was due to be posted overseas to Burma when, shortly before, a bout of food poisoning – ironically on his home visit – had him hospitalised for weeks. In fact it was so serious that his stomach was affected for the rest of his life. By the time he was well enough to be discharged from hospital – and the services – his unit had already gone ... and later suffered massive losses in the Battle of Irawodi against the Japanese.

These experiences had obviously made a great impact on him, for he told these stories with a mixture of wonder and curiosity. And while the whisky may have raised passions and added lustre to other yarns, these wartime memories never altered whether he was sober or not.

After listening to Dad recall those days, I would
jump down from his knee and play soldiers with the
rifle he had carried back from Dunkirk – a long, heavy
weapon handed to him by a Belgian cavalryman during
their flight. I'd shoot imaginary enemies, and puzzle
over why God, whoever he was, would be interested in
my father.

It never occurred to me that this was one and the
same person about whom so much fuss was made each
week. If Saturday nights meant a party without fail, then
Sundays meant church with a fuss. Coming down for
breakfast, the rooms would be stale with the smell of
beer, whisky and cigarettes.

Mum would be struggling to get us all dressed, smart
and ready for morning Mass, while also organising
breakfast and making sure that the Sunday lunch was
ready to go. All the while she was busying herself she
would be grumbling about last night's party and com-
plaining to Dad, who would be nursing a hangover that
screamed for relief, or another drink.

Somehow, though, we would all manage to squeeze
into our best clothes in the nick of time, and march off
solemnly down the road together to St Patrick's, the big,
square redbrick church on the corner.

It's dark, cold and confusing. All the adults sandwiched
in around me, solemn-faced and weary-looking, are
standing and sitting at regular intervals like some sort
of a party game. They are talking, flat-voiced and
disinterested, in a language I don't understand. I know
it's so terribly important to be here – it must be, judging
by the arguments we have making sure we arrive in
good time – but I can't seem to work out why, because
no one seems to be enjoying it.

I'm certainly not; nor, as I squirm to look round,
are any of the adults, as far as I can see. Their faces
seem grey and set, their minds on something other than
what's happening here. Dad's fingers reach out to pinch

me, to stop me from fidgeting, but it only makes me feel even more uncomfortable. How many hours is it since we slid in here, nodding our heads at the altar on the way?

Dad's in an even worse mood than most Sundays because we were a little late setting off. That means we haven't managed to find a space in one of the hard, wooden form rows. In one way I'm glad, because they make me want to wriggle about even more, but that only makes Dad even more annoyed with me. On the other hand, no seat means that we've got to stand up at the back here, hemmed in by all the other latecomers. There is an almost overwhelming aroma of fetid breath and suited bodies, and I feel as though I'm drowning in a sea of tailor's dummies. I'm not tall enough to see what's happening up in the front, and the back-and-forth responses drone on over my head. I crane my head forward as Father Saul approaches and leans towards us; it's worth catching a smell of the pungent incense to stifle some of the other less sweet odours.

At the back of the church on the way out, I look again at that picture of Jesus, similar to the one we've got hanging in all the bedrooms at home. He's looking out in a mournful, wistful sort of way, with two large wounds on the palms of his hands. There seems to be a lot of blood about, and I'm told that he died for me. I don't know how or why, though, and I find the idea rather disturbing. Sometimes I think that he's looking out at me accusingly.

Although it's horribly boring in here, at least it's quiet for a while and there are no rows. It's almost enjoyable for that reason alone. But I know that they'll be falling out again only too soon. In a few minutes – though it seems like days, it's all going to be over again for a week, thank goodness – all the waiting and standing and sitting and looking serious. Then there is going to be a mad rush out of the doors, when all the men disappear in a cloud of cigarette smoke as they light up in unison.

Then Dad and his friends will smile for the first time in the last couple of hours and saunter off down to the pub, while the children will head back home for lunch with Mum. Later there will be more arguments, shouts and confrontations when he rolls home too drunk and too late to eat. She will throw it at him, or the wall perhaps, and there will be screams and scuffles. Then he'll fall asleep until teatime, and as I climb into bed I will look over at that strange picture to see if the blood's stopped flowing yet by any chance. It never has.

The only time I can ever remember church without a fight was at my first communion. Dressed in white robes and sighed over by relatives and family friends, I was chosen to carry the banner in the parade of children receiving the sacraments for the first time, which made Mum very proud. Afterwards there was a party with tea and cakes and soft drinks laid out on trestle tables in the yard behind the church.

There was one bright spot on Sundays, though. After Dad had eaten his lunch – if it was still edible – and slept off most of his lunchtime drinking, he would often take us down to the local cinema, at the bottom of the street. It was a fairly tatty old picture house, but I remember it with great affection because it was one of the few times that we ever did anything together as a family. True we didn't speak to each other and it was dark, but as I sat there in the flickering atmosphere watching the cartoons and features, I used to drink in the sense of closeness, contentment and well-being. I used to wish that I could catch hold of it and take it home with me, but when the final credits had rolled we would head back to the house and reality.

Somehow all the good times seemed to get spoiled. We would make a great effort at Christmas, on St Patrick's

Day and birthdays to enjoy our family celebrations, but
something would always go wrong. I'd invariably end
the day feeling desperately unhappy because what had
begun with such high hopes had ended in arguments
and bitterness again.

Even without visitors and guests – of which there was
an endless stream – ours was a busy house. Yet I still felt
alone and left out. I shared a bedroom with Tony, but
with his being ten years older he didn't have a lot of
time for a baby brother. Sometimes at night I'd be
terrified by the thought that there was a monster lurking
under my bed, just waiting for the right moment to
snake out a tentacle or a scaly hand and drag me under.
I'd call out, and plead with Tony to check that I was safe,
but he'd only jeer and tell me not to be so stupid. At
times the fear was so heavy that I'd pull the sheets high
up over my head and whisper: 'Please, God, don't let
them get me, don't let them get me.' I didn't know who
God was, whether he could hear me, or if he'd have any
interest in helping me should he be listening. But I felt
that I had nowhere else to turn, and my terror made me
clutch at any straw.

I felt closer to my friends than I did my family.
Although my sisters were nearer to my age than Tony,
we never seemed to get on – there were always fights
and rows over what belonged to who, and whether we
were allowed to use it. My best friends were the boys I
played with out on the streets near our home. By the
time I started secondary school, we'd lost the nice,
comfortable house with the garden. Dad's business in-
volvement had turned sour, and he'd lost everything. As
he tried to get another business going, a corner café, we
moved into tatty rented rooms at the top of a private
house on the London Road. This was one of the worst
slum areas of Nottingham, directly across the road from
the county football ground. We always knew when one
of the teams had scored from the roar that went up and
sailed through the windows.

Our family squeezed into the three upstairs rooms, and we shared the bathroom and kitchen with the owner and her son Keith. He was one of my closest mates, and we ran and played together in the street most days. We were careful never to venture too far, though. The crowded, back-to-back houses and alleyways were a maze of small communities, and there were only a few streets within sprinting distance of our front door where it was safe to walk. Go too far afield, and we would get set upon by the local gang for daring to venture onto their territory.

For all the hardships, there was a strong sense of community in the predominantly Irish neighbourhood. This sense of national spirit was important to my parents, whose lives seemed to centre on the weekly gatherings to reminisce and sing the songs they had grown up with. So much so, that when the opportunity came to better ourselves and move on out, it didn't last long.

With conditions being so cramped for our growing family, Dad was one of the first to be offered corporation housing in the Woollaton district, a new suburb being created on the other side of Nottingham. When we moved into our new house, the estate on which it was situated still hadn't been completed. To reach our front door we had to clamber across planks, over the unmade main road.

Although it was the best-equipped and maintained home they had ever lived in, my parents just couldn't seem to settle. They missed the local pubs and the bustling sense of neighbourliness, the nosiness and the squabbles. After just a few months they moved out, and packed us all back to the slumland area – this time into the very heart of the notorious Meadows district. By now Dad's fortunes had improved slightly, and he had managed to get a job as a steel erector on the new power station sites springing up around the region.

The sites were dangerous and demanding places to work. But they suited my father down to the ground. He was made foreman, which meant that he had to keep the hard-drinking, wild migrant workers in check. It was a job that demanded quick thinking, a quick tongue and quick fists. He had all three.

Once he found out that a scaffolder's shoddy work had put an entire team at risk as they worked high up; so he had him sacked. The angry worker – a big, broad Cockney – came down to the Meadows looking for Dad. He found him in one of his favourite locals, and went in to challenge him to a fight. Dad went outside with the man, and laid him cold, flat out on the pavement. When he came round, he took the man back into the pub and bought him a beer. They became good friends.

The good money Dad earned meant that we were able to rent a large, rambling house in Wilford Grove, a tree-lined street from the centre of which you could see the top of Nottingham Castle, cresting the highest point of the hill a couple of miles away. Dad renovated the house from top to bottom, and in addition to throwing the doors open at weekends for parties, we began to take in Irish lodgers who were working in the sites and roads up and down the Midlands.

Among the tenants in our double-fronted home was a cousin who came home drunk one night and got into a violent argument with Mum. It ended with him attacking her and then Tony, who tried to go to her assistance. When Dad came home, he beat the man up savagely and threw him out of the house.

We thought that was the end of it until later that night. With screams and oaths, the man burst through the front door brandishing a wicked-looking butcher's knife. 'I'm going to kill you all,' he screamed in a drunken rage. Dad bundled us all into the front room, and held the door closed as the cousin ranted and swore on the other side. Then he began to attack the door, and I watched in horror as the blade started to break through the thin panelling.

Thankfully, neighbours must have realised that the

commotion was more than the usual and called the police. They arrived just in time to disarm him and bundle him away.

After that, Dad redoubled his efforts to teach me to fight. He'd show me how to punch and guard myself, and insist I repeated the manoeuvres until I'd got them right. He'd also train me repeatedly so that I knew just how to knock someone to the floor with a swift kick of the legs.

'The best way to settle an argument, Johnny,' he would tell me earnestly, 'is to get the first punch in. Worry about the talking afterwards.'

3
Letting Go

Dad's bruising philosophy became the hallmark of my young life. And it was in the second year of school that it exploded in a fashion that was to be repeated – with increasing ferocity – in the years to come.

My first day at school had been fun. Everyone at St Patrick's, the small primary school attached to the local church, made a special effort to make us feel welcome, and I really enjoyed it ... for the last time in my whole school life. I soon discovered that this was not a bright new world opening up in front of me. It quickly became apparent that I was not suited to the academic life.

These days it might even be given a special name and put down to some sort of learning difficulty. Then I was just written off, at an early age, as one of those who wasn't going to go very far. They never actually said so, but I picked it up from the teachers. They took more time and care with some of the brighter kids in the class, while my efforts were hurriedly looked over, if at all.

The feeling of being on the outside of things extended from the classroom into the playground. Although I'd had regular 'lessons' from Dad, I wasn't too confident about getting into a tumble. Photographs of me at the time show that I was smaller than average; and they also capture a pinched expression on my face that I couldn't hide. It was a combination of alienation and fear. The playground scared me; its openness and seeming free-for-all in the rough and tumbles. To make matters worse, the school bully – ginger-haired Mick, who was about two years older – seemed to have antennae that picked up my uncertainty. He regularly singled me out, goading me and making fun of me. I longed to lash out and hurt him, but fear of retaliation kept the anger locked inside, where it brewed quietly.

Then, one day, the pressure became too great – and the lid came off. I'd spent ages in a craft lesson modelling a clay submarine. Not being a scholarly success, I'd been pleased to find something I was fairly good at, and was keen to finish some handiwork that I could take home to show off to Mum. Praise for my schoolwork was rare; this would be a real treat.

The piece had been lovingly finished, and then fired, and I was carrying it carefully home along the streets after school when I turned a corner and came face to face with Mick. He was idling along with some friends in tow. They saw me and came over.

'What have you got there, Goodfellow?'

'Nothing ... I'm just on my way home.'

'You're lying. Come on, let's have a look,' and they forced me to reveal my gingerly-held treasure. As I lifted it up for them to see, Mick whipped a hand forward and shoved, pushing the model out of my hand. It fell onto the pavement and shattered into a dozen pieces. He laughed harshly, as his friends smirked and giggled.

All the bottled-up frustration, loneliness, insecurity and resentment must have escaped in a single, fizzing rush of emotion. I'd never normally have considered taking him on, but I screamed at him: 'You rotten swine, I'm going to kill you for that!'

He looked at me contemptuously and sneered. But his expression turned to bewilderment and then alarm as I balled up my fists and started screaming and lashing out wildly. He jumped back, turned and stumbled away, and even as it all happened in a flash, I sensed a rush of

excitement at the realisation that my unguarded rage
had scared him, and given me the upper hand.

My hands were empty when I got home from school
that day, but I felt as though I'd found something
special. If I just let go and gave my feelings free rein to
express themselves through my fists and feet, then even
the biggest, toughest opponent could be made to listen.
Suddenly I realised that I didn't need to feel intimidated
by anyone else if I was prepared to make sure they had
more reason to fear me.

This lesson made me feel more physically secure in
the playground and on the streets around my home, but
it didn't take away the tension inside. Arguments and
scuffles at home, emptiness and confusion at church,
inferiority and loneliness at school, all combined to leave
me coiled up like a spring.

I can only recall a couple of occasions when that inner
tightness was unwound and replaced by a calm and
peace. They were the summers when my mother took us
over to Ireland to spend some time with her relatives.
We visited members of the family living in and around
Cork, staying with them in little thatched cottages and
running freely in the fields and country lanes. So much
space, fresh air and beautiful countryside was in marked
contrast to the dirty brick streets of the Midlands. We'd
spend hours with our distant cousins, learning how to
trap rabbits, and helping to carry huge baskets contain-
ing packed lunches down to the grown-ups working in
the fields where they were bringing in the harvest.

But then, all too soon, it was back to the big, old house
in Wilford Grove, the weekend parties and the battles in
the home and playground.

Being that much older, big brother Tony had never
really had much to do with the other children in the
family, especially me. If relations with my two sisters
were anything to go by, we probably wouldn't have got
on anyway. Joan was a few years older than me, and I
only ever saw her as competition. She was the one I was

in a contest with over everything: being first to read the weekly comic, getting the best chair in the room, winning the second helping at the dinner table, and most importantly earning the affection of our parents. If family closeness was in short supply to start with, I hated having to share it with anyone else. I wanted to hug it all to myself and savour every last ounce.

So we were always looking for ways to outdo each other, and when Mum and Dad weren't looking, our spiteful teasing and tormenting would quickly give way to full-blooded slaps and punches. As she got older, Joan would tease me in front of her friends when they came round, pushing me about and trying to humiliate me. I responded by making sure that my punches went home hard and hurtfully when we tangled.

I'd already started school by the time Trish arrived, and to begin with she was the much-loved baby of the family. We all helped care for her; I even took my turn feeding her and changing the occasional nappy. I wasn't very good at it, but it made me feel very adult to be trusted with such a responsible job.

Perhaps she took her cues from the examples of her older brother and sister, but as Trish got older she too joined the fighting for first place. As time went on, we began to clash more and more fiercely – worse than I had done with Joan. When Mum and Dad were out, we would dive at each other, fists and feet flying, having driven each other to breaking point. By now I was learning to let the tripwire on my temper go almost at will. The results could be alarming. I had no qualms about striking either of my sisters as hard as I would a schoolground opponent. It didn't make any difference to me that they were girls; they got what they deserved. But on a couple of occasions I frightened even myself when I laid Trish out cold by throwing her against a thick panelled door. I dragged her into the bedroom, opened the window, and with the help of the fresh air managed to bring her round before our parents got back.

By the time I became aware of my emerging sexuality, my attitude towards women – as exemplified by my treatment of Joan and Trish – was already so confused that even a course in human relations would have been hard-pressed to correct my flawed character; much less the crude playground education I received.

A delicious sense of disgust charges through my body, making me tingle, as we head off down the street. I've told my parents that we are going round to a friend's house for a while. It's not a lie, really; only it's not the full story, either.

She's not actually a friend, I suppose. Because if the truth's told we're not really very interested in her as a person at all. We are going for her body, which she seems to get a kick out of feeding to our fascination. I sometimes think that she's using us more than we are using her.

I wonder, too, about what her parents would think if they knew what their daughter was up to in their bedroom while they're out – though we are always careful to cover our tracks. But mostly I don't care. All thoughts seem to get locked away, frozen out, when we are faced with the reality of our schoolboy fantasies.

This is even more unbelievable, exciting and hypno-tising than all the stories we've swapped in the bike sheds, or the men's magazines we've leered over. Since falling into this weekly ritual, my three friends and I have felt strangely older than the other boys in our second-year secondary school group. But there are other emotions, too, spinning away inside.

Even as we arrive at her door, trying to look relaxed in case the neighbours are watching, I know that the sensory overload of the next couple of hours is going to be followed by a flood of shame, guilt and horror; even self-loathing.

Part of me wants to run away from it all – I don't think I'm big enough to cope with all the emotional demands

it makes on me – but the rest just pulls me back
magnetically. I just hope that later I can get in and up to
bed, calling a 'goodnight' from the stairs, without having
to talk to Mum face to face. I don't think I'll be able to
look at her because I'm convinced that she'll know
simply by looking into my eyes all the dreadful things
that have been happening.

I'm also slightly in awe of this thing that seems so
easily capable of dominating my life with a kind of
arrogant ease. Already I'm finding my days and nights
are being swamped by thoughts of sexual activity; there's
scarcely a day goes by when my mind's not running riot.
Just sometimes it's as though I've opened the door of a
lion's cage, and out has roared a beast that's going to
devour me.

But now we have arrived, and I'm lost again in a blur
of anticipated senses. I'll forget about how hollow I'm
going to feel because of the fullness of the moment.

Those early sexual experiences not only scarred me for
future relationships, but they also saw the severing of
the last threads that had held me – albeit tenuously – to
church.

For two years I had served as one of the altar boys at
St Patrick's. My understanding of God – or, rather, lack
of it – hadn't changed in the slightest: he still seemed to
me to be no more than a vague and guilty idea in a few
people's minds. But my serving at the altar thrilled my
parents – it was a note of social standing to have your
youngster hold such an office – and it had also helped
the ordeal of Sunday morning pass more quickly. If I
had to go to church, I figured, I might as well have
something to do to help the minutes along.

So, each Sunday morning, I'd join the other lads with
their close-cropped, slicked-down hair. We'd fight over
who got to wear the cleanest, newest robes – the white
linen shirt and the long, black cassock over the top. We
would put on our most angelic-looking, innocent faces

as we stood solemnly at the front of the church, assisting Father Saul with the mass.

But within a few weeks of starting to experiment with sex, I began to dread having to serve at church. Once the girl with whom my friends and I were meeting came down to our part of the Meadows looking for me. I heard that she was coming and ran inside, closing the door. I didn't come out again until she'd given up the search and gone home. I didn't want anyone to know that I'd been associating with her.

In the same way I dreaded being caught out at church. I sometimes wondered whether Father Saul could read my mind when he looked at me with his gentle, caring eyes. I was horrified at the prospect – the thought that he might know I'd let him down. Having to attend Saturday evening confession with Dad was an awful trial. Waiting to enter the small, screened box, which always smelled strongly of a cocktail of whisky and perfume, my hands would start to sweat profusely and I'd wipe them repeatedly on the sides of my trousers.

Once inside I felt compelled to confess all that I'd done, and my cheeks would burn with shame as I recounted the moments. I hated having to admit the things that my uncontrolled desire had made me do. It left me feeling horribly exposed, and I wondered whether the priest would recognise my voice despite my best efforts to disguise it or, worse, tell my family all I had said.

My experimentation wasn't limited to sex, either. Eager to grow up and leave behind the schoolboy mould into which we felt squeezed, my friends and I also began to dabble in other activities that we reckoned were a sign of maturity beyond our years. With a few pennies each it was possible to scrape together enough money to buy between us a packet of five Woodbines. They were plain, rough cigarettes that roared against the backs of our throats and made our eyes sting as we inhaled. The first few times I tried it, it was all I could do to prevent myself from retching on the spot. Somehow I managed to effect a seasoned sigh of satisfaction as I exhaled between pursed lips.

After a while the level of disagreeability began to drop, and I found myself looking forward to the next smoke snatched – if we were in a brave mood – in a quiet corner of the school, or near to one of the private alleys round our homes. Very soon my liking for nicotine had developed into a craving, and I was finding most of my money going towards the cost of the next packet.

The rest was soon spent on drink. There had always been alcohol around in our home, of course, where it flowed as naturally as tea. My parents had never objected to us having a sip from their glass if we were staying up for one of the weekly parties, but this was different. My friends and I started to smuggle bottles of beer away from our parents' supplies, and then drank them together secretly. I'd already acquired the stomach for alcohol; the taste followed very quickly.

All this rebellious activity fuelled my hatred of authority, which I came to see as personified by anyone connected with school. I loathed every moment of my time at secondary school – a passionate dislike that would not change over the years, even if the reasons for it did.

At first it had been resentment. There had been a good deal of arguing back and forth about whether I should be allowed to attend Trent Bridge Boys' School in the first place. Tucked away at the edge of the Meadows, neighbouring an industrial works and just a few hundred yards from the River Trent, it was a Protestant establishment and so viewed with considerable suspicion.

However, all my closest friends were going there, so I wanted to as well. Finally Mum and Dad gave in and let me go – and from the first day I discovered just why it had a reputation as being one of the toughest schools in the town.

Although I'd learned to take care of myself at primary

school through sheer rage, here I found myself once more at the lower end of the pecking order. The boys in the upper forms were bigger, broader and beefier by far – and determined to make sure that we new pupils knew just what the score was. The first few weeks were a real time of trial for us all. Before and after school, the bigger lads would pick us off and with a brisk roughing over make certain that we knew our place. Favourite tortures were to bend our arms behind our backs and stretch them agonisingly over the metal school railings, or for two more to hold us still while a fourth burned the side of our necks with a lighted cigarette.

I hated the feeling of helplessness before these bullies, and despised them for making me aware of my insecurity. Then, when we were away at a school camp, the chief architect of the fourth formers' reign of terror singled me out for special attention. He began by taunting me and swearing at me, and then started to push me away from the small group that had gathered to watch my humiliation.

'Go on, Goodfellow, get lost, before I beat you up good and proper,' he hissed, pushing me away by the shoulder.

Somewhere inside the trigger went, and I exploded again. I tore into him, grabbed his arms and threw him over my hip as Dad had taught me to do in countless sitting room 'lessons' at home. As he landed on the ground, I dropped on top of him, straddling him with my knees, pinning his arms at his side. And then, methodically and with cool satisfaction, I began to pound his face – right, left – with my fists. He couldn't wriggle free because my weight was pinning him down, and I continued my onslaught with delight until I was finally dragged away by two or three other boys.

It turned out to be the worst possible thing to have done. All the older boys felt slighted that a younger pupil had got the better of one of their classmates. They seemed to think that they each had to take me on to prove their own toughness, and after that I was constantly trying to avoid unnecessary confrontations. One particular time I wasn't quick enough on my feet, and I was cornered and 'branded' by a group of them.

It wasn't so much the pain that enraged me; though it took some time for my singed flesh to heal. More it was the shame and humiliation that seemed to tear a hole deep inside me. I couldn't disguise the blistered record of the attack, no matter how I tried, and I seethed against those who had left me with the visible marks of having been beaten.

Dad didn't seem to worry about all the scrapes I got into at school; many's the time I would return home with skinned knuckles or a bruised cheek. He was more interested in getting a blow-by-blow account of what had happened. Just sometimes I wished he would express some concern or tenderness for me. Instead he quizzed me on how I'd handled myself, and offered tips on what to do the next time it happened.

My standing in the staffroom wasn't too good, either. My inability to absorb information was still there, although a love for reading had somehow kept me in the so-called A stream of school life – by the skin of my teeth. But most of the teachers had little time for me. Their general opinion was that I would never amount to much, and I sensed that I'd been written off as far as they were concerned. 'You'll probably end up in prison, Goodfellow,' one of them told me flatly.

This lack of interest, coupled with their positions of authority, made them prime targets for my fierce hatred. I used to daydream about how I'd like to get my own back on them, particularly when I'd been punished for some misdemeanour or other. Each teacher had his own preferred method, and there were leather straps, bamboo canes and rulers. One teacher in particular used to insist that we held our hand out, palm up, while he administered stinging strokes from a strap. If we pulled our hand away – which was the immediate

painful reaction – then he simply doubled the dosage.
We all loathed him.

My clash with authority came to a head in the metal-
work class in my last year. The teacher was called
Marcisniak; he was a squat, muscular Pole who had
come to Britain during the war and stayed on afterwards. Generally he just ignored me during his lessons,
but on this particular day he came over to see how I was
getting on. I'd been trying to make a brass bowl, and
hadn't done a very good job of beating out the shape,
although I had tried hard. At least I didn't have to
struggle with paper and pen.

Marcisniak ripped into me with criticism. He told me
that I was doing it all wrong, and had to start again and
do it the right way. 'Concentrate this time. Don't be an
idiot all your life, boy!' he snapped.

Being picked out for failing to do the work properly –
despite my best efforts – was bad enough in front of a
workroom full of my friends. But to be ridiculed like
that was too much.

'Don't you call me an idiot!' I shot back.

The teacher reached over and slapped me hard over
the top of the head for answering him back – and the
next thing I knew we were fighting over a bench in the
middle of the class. He screamed and kicked as I tried to
land one really good punch in his face, but he was too
powerful for me and he finally managed to subdue me
with the help of another member of staff who had
rushed in to find out what all the commotion was.

They hauled me off to the headmaster's study, where
I was given a dressing down and threatened with immediate expulsion. I didn't really care if they did throw
me out, but I argued that Marcisniak had started it all
because he'd struck me, and that there was a classroom
of witnesses – my friends – who had seen what had
happened.

The episode seemed to blow over in the days that
followed, but it made me only more keen to leave school

as soon as I possibly could – and for the authorities to see the back of me.

On our last day, we departing fifteen-year-olds were gathered together by the headmaster and given a fatherly pep-talk about going out into the big, wide world and making our way as young men with the future before us. I remember looking over at him as he droned on and thinking with delight that I'd never have to see his smug face again as long as I lived. Walking out of the gates that afternoon, for the last time, was like being released from prison. I felt strangely, euphorically free.

'This is it,' I thought, as I walked home along the streets. 'I've finally made it. No more yes sir, no sir. No more people stopping me from doing what I want to. From now on, people had just better make sure they don't get in my way!'

4
Squaring Up

Three left jabs with my fist smashed into his face almost before he knew what was happening. Another series of blows followed, as inwardly I hoped that someone would step in pretty soon to break up the fight: if they didn't, I was in for trouble.

I was in my late teens, and months working on building sites had toughened me up physically so that my body was as hard as my heart. But Dave was more than a match. He towered over me by about four inches, and must have carried three or four stone more than I onto the scales. I knew that picking a fight with him was asking for problems, but the risk of physical injury was less worrying to me than the danger of losing face. I'd prefer to have mine re-arranged, instead.

The problem was that carpenters thought they were better than those of us who laid bricks, as though their skills were somehow more artistic. It was an un-spoken snobbery that occasionally spilled over into words and violence – such as the morning I tangled with Dave.

We had been working well enough together up until then. I was helping him with his heavy tools bag on a first-floor level at a city-centre building site, when he had to climb down to get some more materials leaving me to wait for his return. Even my toughened arms couldn't hold onto the weight indefinitely, and my grip slackened. Some of his tools slipped out of the side of the bag and tumbled down to the ground, where they crashed against a pile of bricks.

Dave saw the accident and shouted angrily: 'Can't you do anything right, you weakling? I only asked you to hold my bag for a couple of minutes. What a pathetic excuse for a brickie you are.'

His taunt was like a red rag to a bull, and I snapped back: 'Who do you think you're talking to, then, you fat slob?' Peering down at him from above it seemed relatively safe – but the gathering of a small group of lads who had overheard our altercation forced me to climb down, where the scale of my confrontation became more evident. And so without waiting to complete the usual round of oaths, taunts and accusations that would precede a fight, I tore into him with my knuckles.

It took him completely by surprise, and thankfully my gamble paid off. Before Dave could gather his senses enough to come back at me, some of the onlookers had stepped in and pulled me away, while another couple went to Dave to calm him down and defuse the situation.

I was prepared to face the prospect of being hurt because I was determined not to lose the sense of identity I had discovered, for the first time, since starting-work on the building sites. People recognised my abilities, and respected my character, and I was almost prepared to kill to make sure I didn't lose that standing; that sense of personal value and worth. It didn't allow for people – of any size – attempting to belittle or taunt me in front of others.

It was hard work on the sites, but I felt that I belonged; that I fitted in. It was something I hadn't experienced before – at home, at church, or at school – and I valued the feelings of purpose and position. Particularly as early experience on leaving school had shattered my initial dreams of working life as an adult.

Despite my academic failings, I'd somehow managed to secure a job as a trainee inspector at a small, grey engineering factory on the other side of town, a twenty-minute bus ride away. It soon became apparent to me that I was once again a small, inconsequential fish in a big pool. I hated being the butt of the older men's jokes and taunts, and singled out as 'the new lad'.

My supervisors quickly realised, too, that I wasn't really capable of grasping all the things an inspector apparently needed to know in a factory that turned out brass rings by the thousand. After a few weeks I was unceremoniously downgraded, and put to work on a capstan lathe. I was embarrassed and humiliated, sure that everyone in the place knew I wasn't up to the job I had been given originally – unaware that most of them probably didn't even know my name, and cared about that fact even less. Somehow even the sequences of lathe operation were too much for me, though. Next I found myself handed a plain brown overcoat and a brush. I was at the bottom of the pile, reduced to mundane labouring jobs – sweeping the floors, moving heavy loads of metal from one end of the factory floor to the other, and brewing tea.

This rapid slide confirmed all my worst fears. I felt stupid, worthless and despised. To make matters worse there was no one I could turn to, because I couldn't bring myself to tell my parents. They still thought I was a trainee inspector, and I'd pass over their occasional questions about how things were going with a deliberately vague answer, or attempt to change the topic of conversation. I couldn't bring myself to admit that I had failed, and I feared my father's scorn for not making the grade.

So for a year or so I simply had to endure it quietly, spending my time daydreaming about sex, or how I'd like to get my own back on all the people who seemed to be squashing me down. I wove violent fantasies of revenge and lust that somehow only managed to make the mundane reality around me seem even more infuriating.

Eventually I handed my notice in and managed to

convince Mum and Dad that I'd left because there weren't enough prospects for me at such a small firm. If only they knew!

For a couple of months I kicked my heels trying to find new work. While I was still at school I'd toyed with the idea of following my brother, Tony, down the pit. I knew that life underground could be dangerous – he'd been off work the best part of a year at one stage, recovering from a cave-in that had damaged his back. But I still fancied the idea of becoming a miner – until we went down a pit on a school visit. The heat, dirt and darkness hundreds of feet below were alarming, and I left my romantic thoughts of attacking the black seams behind me when we returned to the surface.

Then, one day, I decided to try my hand at brick-laying – and found myself a new identity. I was apprenticed to a local firm, Costain and Sons, who were contracted to build on the big city-centre development sites in Nottingham. I soon discovered that here, at last, I'd found something I was good at. In a strange way I felt free for the first time that I could recall.

A cold, crisp morning and my steamy breath rolls away in a cloud as I blow on my hands. There's an art to laying bricks well. It's all to do with touch and feel, so gloves are out. After a few weeks your fingers become toughened up, though, and you get used to the cold. Sometimes the temperature drops so low that we have to spend the first minutes of the day chipping the ice off the bricks that have been left out overnight.

Up on the higher levels you get a fine view of the city. It's really warming to walk out to the edge of the building, way up high, and look down on the crowds of people scurrying to a day in the office. This is a man's world, rough and tough. It's good to be accepted as one of the blokes, and to share a coarse joke or guffaw as a young girl blushes and hurries away from one of our rooftop wolf-whistles.

I also enjoy the sense of achievement and satisfaction – something I could never find in all the days I struggled with books and pens. I appreciate the adept way I have learned to 'roll the board' – cutting off a fresh slab of cement, and slapping it down on top of a row of bricks so that it spreads along a couple of feet. Then I smear it out flat so that the next row of bricks lie level as they are placed carefully and firmly on top. Next comes 'buttering the edge' – running a spread of cement up the side of each brick to be laid, so that they are mortared to the next one in line.

They say that a good brickie can lay a thousand bricks a day, and I'm just topping that total. I know that I'm appreciated because I'm always given the best jobs, and I push myself hard to make sure that no one else manages to knock me off my top spot. Sometimes, standing above everyone else on a high work point, that's just how I think of myself, and I love the sense of importance, of being someone!

The long hours of climbing, stretching and carrying have wound a steely thread into my body, and I relish the sense of power and strength. I'm fitter and stronger than I can ever remember, and this awareness heightens my readiness to let go with a punch or two. I'm not someone to tangle with lightly.

The guys on the site are also a good bunch of people to work with – family, in a strange way. We swear and fight and try to outdo each other, but there is most of the time a feeling that we're all in it together. I like being a part of something. It's new.

My employers soon spotted that I had a natural talent for the job, and teamed me up with one of their most experienced men. The old-timers in turn, responded warmly to my efforts and took me under their wing, in a way.

My apprenticeship involved a four-year course with day training sessions at a local college. I was working towards my City and Guilds certificate in bricklaying, but the freedom and achievement I'd found on the site only compounded the sense of inadequacy I experienced back in the classroom. The college kicked me out after eighteen months, for being too rebellious and argumentative – which included a study room brawl with another young apprentice who had dared to criticise my practical work on one occasion.

Because my abilities won me the respect of the older men, I was spared some of the treatment handed out to newcomers. There was a definite pecking order on a site, and everyone held their place with threats and abuse and – when it was needed – violence. Many of the guys on the crews were fresh out of prison, too, and they brought an extra sense of aggression and anger to the arguments that would take place. 'You learn inside never to back down to anyone,' one of them told me one day.

My good standing on site brought my dad's admiration for the first time – but he showed it in a strange way. Maybe it was because of the way he had to keep the young men in his construction gangs in line; anyway, he turned to fighting.

There had been many scuffles and tussles in the past, and the prospect of a real battle had bubbled for a long time. After I'd been at work for a few months, I decided that Mum and Dad couldn't make me go with them to church on Sunday mornings any more. So when Dad's voice came roaring up the stairs telling me to get up and get dressed, I ignored him, rolled over and went back to sleep.

A few minutes later he thundered up, crashed through the door and barked at me: 'Johnny, I just told you to get up. It's almost time for church, and we are not going to be late, by God . . .'

I rolled over and peeked over the top of the sheets. 'I'm not going any more, Dad,' I told him flatly.

'You what!' he exploded. 'Don't you think you can

tell me what you are and aren't going to do ... just get yourself downstairs straight away!' And with that he stormed out and stomped downstairs again. I continued to lie there, tensing myself for another confrontation, and a few minutes later heard the front door slam as Mum and Dad and the girls set off for St Patrick's.

Dad and I never talked about that confrontation again, but he would always glare at me at lunchtime when I'd finally surface after a good, long lie-in. As well as welcoming the escape from the insufferable boredom and choking guilt that used to swamp the hours I spent at church, I was secretly thrilled because I'd stood up to Dad and he had not been able to face me down. I sensed that it was the beginning of the end of his domination of me.

He must have been aware of this shift in our relationship, too, because after I started bricklaying he began to try to provoke me into a full-scale fight ... especially on nights when he'd had a few too many drinks down at one of the locals. He would come home and try to spur me into a brawl: 'Come on Johnny, my lad, let's see what you're made of,' he would say, inviting me forward with a wave of his left hand – his right held up to his chin in a boxer's stance.

Usually I would walk out of the room or wave him away and say: 'Oh, come on, I don't want to fight you, Dad. That's stupid ...'

One night he continued to bait me. 'Are you frightened of me, or something?' he asked as we stood close by, near the door. I didn't even get round to answering. The next thing I knew my head had exploded in a galaxy of bright stars, and I was lying spread backwards across the kitchen table. Dad had sent me sprawling with a right hook to the chin.

The inner safety catch went again, and with a scream I came to my feet. In a burst of raw anger I grabbed him by the lapels and slammed him backwards against

the wall, almost lifting him off his feet. Then I threw
him down into a chair, bent his head back and snarled
into his face: 'If you ever do that again ... I will kill
you.'

I truly meant it – and he knew. All the anger, hurt and
bitterness I felt I'd stored up over the previous years
came out in that simple threat. For a brief moment there
was a flicker of uncertainty, perhaps even fear, in his
eyes.

It was a sweet moment of bitterness.

5
Easy Money

The stale, foul smell stole into my nostrils and slid down to the back of my throat where it seemed to curl into a ball and threatened to make me gag. I wished that I didn't recognise it.

Gingerly I opened one eye a fraction to investigate, careful not to allow too much harsh light to spill through into my head. It felt as though it had been put through a blender, and too much brightness would have sent me retching.

Looking across from where I lay, I could make out a plain, grey wall, and as I looked up ... the source of my nausea. Smeared across from left to right as far as I could see was dark human excrement. I groaned and clenched my teeth to try to stop my stomach from rebelling against this revolting start to the day.

My sluggish efforts to piece together just where I was and what I was doing there were abruptly halted as the light seemed to fade. A large shape thrust into my face, and I could gradually make out the form of a square human head. Rancid breath blew into my face as this unshaven, sweaty countenance peered at me.

'What have they got you in for then?' the voice demanded in a flat tone.

The question brought bits and pieces of information tumbling into place. This man was sharing the cell into which I had been pitched the night before after my abortive attempt to escape from the police. The realisation only added to the feeling of sickness deep inside.

'Err, theft ... they caught me breaking into a jeweller's shop in the town centre ... how about you?'

'Rape.'

Shocked, I sat up and backed against the wall at the side of the bunk, trying not to show that I was alarmed. Far better if he thought that I was a police cell regular, rough and tough and used to looking after myself behind bars.

Fortunately I was saved from having to try to make any further conversation by a rattling at the heavy iron door set in the far wall. It swung open slowly, and a short-sleeved policeman stepped through holding a mug of tea that he set down at a small, scratched table before giving me a disinterested look and disappearing again. The thick door swung to and closed with an air of finality. I sipped the warm, weak tea and ran my fingers through my untidy hair.

My previously smart blue suit was crumpled and creased; my mouth felt as though a crowd of maggots had been sleeping in it; and my stomach pitched and turned like a cork on a wave. An awful aroma clung to my clothes and hair. So this was how my high-living Friday night out had ended.

It had started like so many others, full of hopes for a few hours of wild excitement. Besides earning an identity and feeling of worth for myself working on the sites, I'd also found out what it meant to have plenty of money to throw around. Working hard to pump down my thousand bricks a day, I was soon bringing home top money. The small brown envelope that was slapped down into my waiting palm every Thursday was always satisfyingly full. At least, for a while.

Alcohol was by now second nature, and I naturally responded to the hard-drinking habits of the older men around, whose consumption I was easily able to match. There would be a pint or two at lunchtime and a few more each night down at the local, but it was at the weekend when the serious socialising would begin.

Hurrying down a big cooked tea, I'd be washed and changed and out of the house early on Friday evening. A stroll down the road and I'd sink a couple of pints with the neighbours before straightening my tie and sauntering on into town to one of the busy bars near the city centre. The Flying Horse was a favourite; always seeming to be packed with more people and noise than the room could comfortably take. There would be a swirl of laughs and drinks and tall stories and more drinks.

The lads would gather there and swap stories about the week, or discuss the prospects of female company in store at the dance hall later on. Later in the evening we would drift on to Yates' Wine Lodge, a place for some serious drinking. With its sawdust covered flooring, large mirrored walls and cast-iron ceiling poles, it looked like the deck of a ship stripped bare and tied down in prospect of a storm. That wasn't far from the truth, in some ways, because as the alcohol loosened tongues, ties and fists, fights would break out as the night wore on. We'd ignore the old Irishmen sitting in the corners with their wives, swapping even older stories about the homeland, and stand in a circle in the centre of the room, downing drink after drink and daring anyone even to consider pushing through us on the way to the bar.

Finally it would be on to the Locarno or one of the other big dance halls, great big aircraft hangars of places with wall-to-wall bars and large dance floors where the girls shuffled around together in time to the strains of the resident band, waiting to be chatted up by one of the leery men standing around at the side eyeing up the talent.

Not surprisingly, this kind of living soon saw off even my healthy wage packet. The fact that I'd gamble over three-card brag during my weeknight pub nights down in the Meadows, coupled with my drinking and dancing appetite, meant that my money never lasted the whole week – sometimes not more than a few days.

So it had been last night. I'd slipped out of the club a little after 2 am, and with only a handful of small change had no option but to start the five-mile walk home. The music and drink were still humming round my veins as I strolled drunkenly down the main shopping area, looking at all the window displays and feeling sorry for myself that I never seemed to have enough money. I couldn't even afford a coat, I bemoaned, as I pulled my thin jacket closer around me in an effort to keep out the early morning cool air.

I'd already turned to crime to finance my lifestyle, with no sense of guilt or wrongdoing. One of the easiest scenes to be made was at the dance hall. A friend and I would choose a couple of girls and get talking. When they slipped off to dance – they always went in pairs, giggling – we'd rifle their handbags and take out the purses. Then we'd slip off to the gents, take out any money, dump the purses in the water cistern, and disappear into another part of the club. We reckoned that if we weren't going to get a girl into bed, we might as well at least get her money.

It seemed to me generally that other people had more than they needed, and I didn't have enough. It was as simple as that – and I also savoured the notion of getting something for nothing. It was as though I was getting my own back on the world that seemed to be against me.

When stealing and violence can be combined, it's even more satisfying. Bob and I are down to our last half pint in a scruffy Meadows pub, with pay day a lot of drinking time away, when I suggest that we simply just empty our glasses and go out and find ourselves the cost of the next round – at someone else's expense.

It's dark as we shuffle back into the shadows of an alleyway a few streets away, within shouting distance of my home. All we can hear is our own shallow breathing as we wait, straining to catch the sound of an approaching step. Someone's coming ... a cough and a shuffle; it sounds like a man, maybe on his way home from a quiet drink down the local with his friends. Or perhaps he's heading home after working overtime. Either way, his pockets should have a few pounds in them.

Half-nervous and half-thrilled at the audacity of what we're going to do we wait until the last moment -- and then spring. 'You, give us your money or there's going to be trouble.' Menacing tones and threatening glares that can be clearly understood despite the dark. But this target isn't easy. Crack! He's caught Bob with a blow to the face and it's all starting to go wrong. With the desperation of fear at being identified we redouble our efforts. The man crumples into the ash of the pathway under our combined attack.

He's screaming and shouting for help, and the hairs on the back of my neck are standing on end as I expect half the neighbourhood to turn out of their houses at any moment. 'Shut up, man!' I snarl, kicking him in the face with the toe-end of my boot. This silences him and he curls into a ball, holding his battered face.

We jerk him over onto his side, and rifle his pockets angrily. There doesn't seem to be much, but there's no time to hang around. Only after we've sprinted a couple of roads away do we stop to count our pickings. Two pounds. Just enough for a few drinks each. There's the faint sound of an ambulance siren as we saunter back into the pub we left about half an hour ago.

It's great to share a private joke as we lean over the bar and ask for two pints of best bitter, please. This violent draught tastes great, and we savour it and the excitement of the last few minutes. 'What do you mean, is everything all right?' I ask one of the old chaps who has wandered over to see us again. Why is he asking?

I follow his gaze and look down. Fresh splotches of spilled blood are still clearly visible down the front of my trousers.

'Oh that, it's nothing. We just ran into a little bit of trouble down the road a way, didn't we, Bob?'

'Oh, that, yeah, that's right. Just a little bit of trouble. But we sorted it out all right. Isn't that right, Johnny?'

'Yeah. Cheers!'

And we giggle through the foamy head of the ale.

My mental gears started to whirr again as I weaved my way past the large-fronted jeweller's shop on the corner. A galaxy of rings, brooches and watches twinkled out at me from the brightly-lit display boards. Almost before I knew what I was doing, I had run over to the roadworks just in front of the shop, picked up a heavy red road lamp in which flickered a candle, and began to pound the metal case against the thick glass frontage.

I swung with all my might two, three times. Then, with my fourth attempt, the glass shattered and fell in. Quickly I threw the lamp to one side and, stepping up, jumped into the display space at the front of the shop. I ignored the shrill alarm that had begun shrieking as soon as the glass gave way, and started stuffing my pockets full of everything I could lay my hands on.

Rings, tie-pins, watches, ear-rings, bracelets, brooches, necklaces – they all were scooped up frantically as I tore items off display trays and scattered others aside to grab what I wanted. It was a thrill to snatch these valiable items up and know that they were mine for the taking.

With my two jacket pockets bulging, chains trailing out the top, I grabbed a handful of other display cards to my chest and jumped down from the window, turning to my right up a side street. As I ran away up the pavement, trinkets dropping to the ground all around, a roaring laugh of pleasure broke from my throat. This was marvellous. My previous crimes seemed tame and timid in comparison! I was already planning my next break-in.

But the moment was shortlived. I hadn't got more than a couple of hundred yards up the road when I heard the unmistakable bee-bah of a police patrol van behind my shoulder, pulling up outside the shop. Panic! For all my careful observations before I'd attacked the shop, I must have missed a late-night walker somewhere nearby who had seen my crime.

'He went up that way ... there he is!' The cry pumped adrenalin into my heart, and I picked up my legs and tore off up to the top of the street. At the end I ran round a low wall and into the wide churchyard of St Nicholas, one of the oldest churches in the city. My elation had given way to cold fear, and I crouched down behind a large black tombstone with my heart beating wildly inside my chest. It had all happened too quickly. How had the police managed to arrive at the scene so fast? They'd ruined my moment!

As my breath came in great sobs, I threw the display cards away across the tombstones, where they scattered and rolled, tinkling.

In a half-crouched position, I peered round the side of the gravestone. Thankfully there were no street lights close by, so I was still in some shadow. I could just see the police van pulling up to a halt at the side of the road, and the officer in the passenger seat staring out through the side window with intense concentration.

Careful to keep low so as not to be spotted, I scurried away behind the tombstones and monuments to another wall at the rear of the churchyard. I'd just made my way to the top of a steep drop of steps that would lead me down to a street forty feet or so below – and probable safety – when I heard dogs barking, and a cry.

'There he is! Hey, you, stop. This is the police.'

The shout startled me, and as I turned I lost my footing and tumbled down the steps, cracking my head and ripping my clothes as I went. But the fear was an anaesthetic, and at the bottom I picked myself up without even stopping to think about the bruises, and lunged off through an alleyway and out into another main street.

At first I thought I'd managed to lose them, but then a couple of hundred yards up the street I heard another shout from behind.

'Oi, you, stop – or we'll let the dogs go.'

I slowed to a halt, my chest heaving from the chase. I knew it was pointless trying to outrun the police dogs, so I turned to face my pursuers in the grip of fear, frustration and anger. The last few minutes' physical exertion seemed to have washed some of the alcohol from my brain and I was already thinking fairly clearly again. What had I done? What had I let myself in for? I'd never been caught before. What would my parents say? How could I face it if people found out?

The two policemen didn't appreciate their chase, clearly. The one in front came over and pushed me hard in the chest, backing me up against the wall of an office complex. 'You stupid kid, what the hell do you think you've been doing, eh? You've really gone and landed yourself in it for this, I'm telling you.'

He spun me round and pushed my face up against the rough brick, while he pulled my arms behind me and clicked the handcuffs into place. 'You didn't really think you were going to get away with it, did you? You've just gone and made things worse for yourself, that's all.'

Still swearing angrily at me, they dragged me to their van and threw me in the back, where I was separated from the dogs by only a wire partition. The Alsatians barked and snarled at me through the wire throughout the bumpy journey back to the police cells, and fear of the dogs and anger at myself and the police drove me to smash my fists repeatedly against the inner wall behind the driver's head.

'Let me out of here, you pigs!' I screamed. 'I hate you coppers, I hate you!'

I was bundled out of the van fairly roughly, and manhandled through the booking-in procedure and down into one of the filthy cells beneath Nottingham's guild hall. With a parting warning that they'd remember my face and I'd better watch my back in the future, the policemen slammed the door shut and left me in the dark.

Trapped and in a rage, I pounded the wall a couple of times with my hands before throwing myself full-length onto the bunk, covered only with a thin, old blanket, and falling into a heavy, despairing sleep.

I had just finished replaying these events in my befuddled mind the following morning when another policeman opened up the cell door and stuck his head round.

'Goodfellow, come on out. Your old man's here for you upstairs.'

I followed him uncertainly. I was dirty, uncomfortable and hungry. I hoped that he'd sorted things out and come to take me home. I found out the reason for his visit as soon as I stepped into the small interview room at the top of the stairs.

He lunged across at me from the other side of the room, throwing one punch after another. 'What on earth do you think you've been up to, boy?' he demanded. 'I never brought you up to become a little thief, did I? Is that all you can think of to repay your poor mother after all these years?'

Dad continued to shout and rant as three police officers pulled him away and sat him down in a chair, urging him to be calm and to collect his thoughts. Everything was going to work out. He looked up at me with anger and shame in his eyes – and then crumpled. Falling forwards and dropping his head into his hands he began to weep. 'Oh son, oh son,' he cried.

I just stood there over by the opposite wall, looking down at the ground and squirming inside. I didn't feel sorry for him – but I was horribly embarrassed. I didn't know which was worse – that my dad should try to beat me up instead of wanting to take me home, or that he'd burst into tears.

It was to be another three days before the police finally let me out on bail – time in which I grew accustomed to the stench and dirtiness of the place. But I never could come to terms with the sense of grievance

I felt. It didn't really occur to me that I'd got the just deserts for my criminal actions. I just felt sick that the police had caught me.

Going home was dreadful. Dad shouted and swore again, and Mum burst into tears and wrung her hands. They were scenes to be repeated when my fine, costs and two-year suspended prison sentence were handed down at the magistrates court a few weeks later – and reported for all the neighbours to see in the local paper.

For a while this encounter with the law brought me to my senses. I restricted myself to one or two trips a week down to the locals, where I'd play cards or dominoes with the old men. But pretty soon I slipped back into my old ways, and once again I was finding that the money I could earn legitimately wasn't enough. I decided, though, that I'd stick to crimes that were less likely to get me caught.

I returned to cars, which were one of my favourite targets. It was easy, walking along the road late at night, to casually try the handles of a few of the vehicles parked along the way. And it was amazing how many motorists didn't seem to check the locks properly before leaving. Often I found one of the doors open, and was able to dart in and rush away with a coat, a cassette player, or some tools. I'd sell them to friends for a couple of pounds, and that would finance the next round or two.

One late night I went spying on all the cars left in a temporary car park on a derelict site round the back of the town centre. In the rear of one I saw a whole pile of brand new jeans. I guessed that the driver must be a travelling salesman, and these his samples. None of the doors were open, but with a handy brick I'd soon shattered the rear window and carried the jeans off in a suitcase conveniently left behind, too.

By this time it was about 3 am, and as I walked down towards the station with my booty, I came across a policeman strolling along the pavement. Thinking quickly

to avoid suspicion, I went over to him and enquired
when the next train left for Derby. My forwardness
must have disarmed him, even if it was strange for a
young man in a smart blue suit to be carrying a bulging
suitcase round the empty streets in the early hours of
the morning.

'Oh, it goes out at about six,' he told me brightly.

'Thanks, officer. I'll go in and wait,' I replied.

And I did. After a couple of hours' sleep I caught the
train to Derby, the nearest Midland industrial town of
any size, and once there headed for the building sites.
Even at a pound a pair for top quality jeans, I knew that
there would be no questions asked. Within a couple of
hours I'd sold my entire 'stock', and the case into the
bargain. I returned to Nottingham with empty hands
and a bulging wallet, and a private sense of pride at what
I'd been able to get away with.

I looked around at the other people in the carriage – a
young mother, a schoolboy, a solicitor type, and a couple
of shop assistants – and wanted to laugh at them for
their safe, respectable suburban lives. If only they knew
what I was up to.

6

On the Edge

I had returned from my first visit to Spain. A friend and I had left our bricklaying jobs in the middle of the summer holiday season and travelled over to the continent to investigate the claims we had heard about life on the Costa Brava. We'd left it rather too late to get fixed up with good posts, though, and after just a couple of weeks we returned to England. My time in Spain had been enough to open my eyes to the possibilities, however, and going back to laying more rows of bricks seemed horribly tame.

I enjoyed my drinking, and a fight was the perfect way to finish an evening, but I'd never have considered that I was in danger of losing control. It just seemed to me that I needed more excitement, more stimulation than the average guy in his boring, nine-to-five world. So when an old site friend called me one day and asked whether I fancied joining the steeplejack trade, I jumped at the chance.

Basically, you got paid a lot more for doing the same job as a bricklayer – only higher up. The firm I joined had contracts for repairs and maintenance on industrial chimneys all over the Midlands – big, redbrick fingers that poked anywhere between 80 and 200 feet into the sky.

I thought it was fantastic. Here was the excitement I'd been craving, the thrill that could keep me charged up through the day until it was evening and time to go down the pubs again. I was apprenticed to one of the most experienced jacks, Ted, and he soon had me shinning up and down the sides of these chimneys as though I'd been doing it all my life. It was my job to run up and down bringing Ted's tools, and the ten-foot lengths of laddering he needed to lay a climbing route up the side of the chimney. When he'd climbed halfway up the highest section, he'd turn and balance with his back against the rungs. Then he'd reach his arms down to take the next section as I passed it up to him, swing his arms up over his head and hook the next section up. It took ice-cool nerves and catlike balance, but he made it all seem as easy as hanging out the washing. I loved his casual style, and relished getting to the top.

Our job at the top of the chimney would invariably be to replace worn and damaged brickwork. That would involve fixing up a hanging platform that we'd sit on beside the top of the chimney. Then we'd knock away the bricks before reaching the most crucial part; removing the wire band that held the chimney in. Even the most experienced jacks would take a deep breath before this part of the job, because you were never sure how much tension would be released when the metal sheet was cut through: it could potentially jump back and pitch you off your small seat.

During the months I worked with Ted – travelling all over the country, staying in bed-and-breakfast accommodation and enjoying the drama of the work high above the skylines – there were a number of incidents involving other men in the company. One jack was hurt when he slipped because a ladder section hadn't been properly hammered home, and another actually died when he toppled from the highest point of a factory chimney.

These reports didn't put me off, though. They just emphasised the danger of what I was doing, and I'd mention these incidents to my friends down the pub as though they endorsed my bravery and devil-may-care attitude. Until one day.

We'd been working on an eighty footer at a hospital site, and reached the top. The chimney was still in use, and we could see the warm air shimmering over the hole as we got level with it; a sign every jack hated. Because of the width of the hole at the top, we could only manage to secure the bosun's chair – which could hang from chains stretched across the aperture – by inching round the narrow lip to the other side.

Sitting astride the lip, I began to scoot my way carefully round to the other side. I was halfway there when my sense of confidence and security suddenly drained away just as though someone had pulled a plug out of the bottom of my foot. The ground to my right seemed to leap up at me, and the deep black hole to my left felt as though it was sucking me down. I became aware of the heat rising up and rippling over my leg and side, and shook my head as pictures of me tumbling down, head over toe, raced around in my mind. I froze, gripping the brick wall as tightly as I had ever held anything. I closed my eyes and tried to wish myself down to the ground and safety.

My stillness was shattered by shouts and angry cries from down below. Ted was furious, and thought I was larking around, delaying him. Anger at his lack of concern together with fury that he'd witnessed my failure rose and sparked me into moving. I reached round, tore the chains and fittings from their place and hurled them down to the ground. Then, without looking back, I swung a leg backwards over the ladder and climbed down to earth. Ted was waiting at the bottom, hands on his hips and a sharp word on his tongue. I ignored him.

'That's it, I've had enough. I'm leaving. Today. *Now*,' I told him, turning and walking away from the chimney. I didn't care if I never saw another ladder in my life.

I decided that thrills were better if they were found at other people's expense, and turned my attention back to the pubs and the closing-time pavements, for I knew that I only had a couple of months or so to go until I'd be able to head out to Spain once again, only this time with a full-season job lined up.

The Crazy Horse Saloon gave me everything I was looking for. As much drinking, fighting and sex as I could consume, with no costs and no one to answer to. And while all this was going on, I was quietly hiding away as much money as I could. I sometimes used to wonder if I could possibly stash away any more money under the grubby mattress of my bunk without anyone getting too suspicious. So I just trusted that the other guys were, like myself, generally too tired, too drunk, or too stoned to have much time for observation tests.

That summer was a turning point. While previously I'd been able to run wild and yet still manage to rein myself in enough to complete a good day's work, I returned to Nottingham completely blown away. My summer of excess had ruined me for what now seemed to be very ordinary, everyday life.

To start with, I resented having to pay for my drinks! Having enjoyed a summer when the beer and Bacardi had been free and plentiful, I'd not realised how dramatically my consumption had rocketed – nor what demands that would make on my pocket. I quickly found the savings I had returned with being poured over the counter in the pubs and clubs.

Physically I was in bad shape, too. Heavy drinking and poor diet had taken their toll, and I'd lost the wiry condition site work had got me into. I was exhausted after just a couple of hours of bending and straightening and carrying bricks. I had a hangover until lunchtime, and getting up to be at work by 8 am was like a dreadful punishment.

At lunchtime I would go down to the nearest pub for a few pints to try to keep me going. As often as not, though, it would turn into an afternoon's binge, and I would simply not go back to work. My reputation among the foremen wasn't good, and such absences meant that my pay packet would be slimmer at the end of the week.

It all seemed to be a downward spiral, and one that I readily ascribed to some organised discrimination against me. What I didn't admit to myself was that in addition to being an alcoholic, I was by now a full-blown drug addict too. Such huge quantities of speed and hash had been consumed during the months in Spain that my body seemed to burn without it. I managed to find a few contacts in some of the scruffier bars in Nottingham, but it never seemed to be as readily available as at the Crazy Horse Saloon.

When I couldn't get hold of the drugs I desperately wanted to help me recapture the buzz I'd known, I would find myself going into dark, deep depressions. Never being particularly sociable at the best of times, I would sink into myself. At times like this it seemed as though the most ordinary attempt at making conversation was a physical attack. I'd avoid talking to people, remaining at the bar with my solo drink, or disappearing to my room at home. Family relationships had hit an all-time low on my return. My family were visibly shocked and concerned about my condition, but I'd closed down any efforts to talk with them about what had happened. I simply used their home like a hotel; somewhere to lay my head before stumbling out in search of another drink or another blast of dope.

The offer of work in Switzerland seemed like a lifeline to a drowning man. It came completely out of the blue that autumn – a letter from some friends who had been working at the Crazy Horse Saloon and who knew someone opening a new hotel in the fashionable ski resort of Hoyt Nandes, near Sion. Would I join them as a waiter?

The Bluesy Hotel turned out to be nothing like the Crazy Horse Saloon. Well built, tastefully appointed and well decorated, it was intended to be a haunt for the wealthy and particular. Soon after arrival I found myself starting French lessons so that my serving style would match my sharp uniform. It was a far cry from what I was used to, but I enjoyed this new world in a strange way, and threw myself into learning how to enquire after Monsieur's choice of wine, and how best to serve a dish to Madame.

In addition to waiting on tables in the small restaurant, I was put in charge of the coffee shop and bar. Such responsibilities suited me down to the ground. I may have been enjoying the new job I had, but that didn't stop me from trying to rob my employer blind. With him so trusting, it was an easy thing to take over a bottle of the best red for a client, take his money and then somehow forget to ring it up at the bar. Fairly soon I had another small mountain of money piling up in my room.

My plan was to amass as much as I could in a fairly short time, and then simply to disappear. But before I could pull all the loose ends together, a beat-up old camper van pulled into the car park one night and out hopped two American travellers who were passing through the area.

Harvey and his friend were students, taking some time out from their studies to see Europe. Money was running low, so they were looking for work that would help tide them over. By now I was also running the disco and the restaurant because my two friends had found the quietness of the hotel scene too much and left. I took Harvey and his mate on.

That night as we chatted in my room, Harvey reached into his travel bag. The words dried up on my lips and my mouth dropped open, as he pulled out one well-wrapped parcel after another. It was the biggest haul of hash I had ever seen – enough to keep a dealer in the lap of luxury for years back in England. Just seeing the drug seemed to set my juices flowing, and I licked my lips as he peeled the plastic covering off the greeny-brown substance and smiled: 'Ever tried this, then, Johnny?'

Then he broke off a big chunk, crumbled it, and we

rolled it into a few cigarettes. The rest of the night
passed in a delightful haze of warm, cotton-wool feelings as the drug flowed through my bloodstream like a
welcome old friend.

The pattern was set. Pretty soon we were smoking for
breakfast, lunch, tea and supper, and the days seemed
to disappear in a blur of late nights—talking, laughing
and smoking. We raced through the dull days of serving
the dinners so that we could get to the next hash time.
For in addition to the physical pleasure, I sensed that I
was on the edge of something else.

The blue-grey smoke of our latest joint curls away lazily
up to the ceiling, like a corkscrew. I watch it rather
dreamily, and think how the hash is unplugging the
cork in me, and that bottled up inside there's something
rich and rare, a vintage! Over the past few days I feel
that I've suddenly been let in on what may be one of the
biggest and best-kept secrets in the world. There's more
to life!

I inhale slowly and deeply, sucking the hash right
down to my toes. Mellow is the right word for this stuff.
I feel warm and relaxed and comfortable, rather like an
old slipper. And it makes me feel free and creative as the
notes of music from my cassette player ring crystal clear.

'You see, man . . .' and a long, studied silence. 'It's all
about finding yourself. You've got to find yourself –
where you've come from, where it's all at. D'you know
what I mean?' he squints at me, with one eye closed,
through the smoke.

'Yeah, Harvey,' I nod. 'I think I do. Tell me some
more.' I'm not actually sure that I do know what he's
talking about, but the way he says it and the earnestness
with which he talks convinces me it must be right. It
sounds good; like there's something around, maybe just
beyond my view at the moment, to which I can belong,
where I won't be left out. Something I can find and be
part of. The prospect excites me in a way that drinking,

fighting and sleeping around never have. It's a curious sensation, and one that I want to last.

And then the mood washes away, changing, and we're giggling fit to bust over a nonsense incident from the day. The dope seems to bring all my emotions to the surface in a way I've never really known before; all the feelings other than anger, resentment, jealousy, rage and aggression. It's like someone's plugged up the sink and left the tap running. The water rises and rises, and then suddenly it splashes over the sides, flowing down.

Other times it would be my taste buds that seemed to be exploding in scale, and I developed a sudden, ravenous appetite. So we would tiptoe down to the hotel larder, sneak away with ten or a dozen bars of chocolate and gorge ourselves on them, revelling in the sticky sweetness of it all. Only the next morning I'd have a bit of a headache and feel slightly nauseous, unsure whether it was because of the food or the drugs. I preferred to think it was the sweets, as I didn't want to believe that anything which could make me feel so wonderfully relaxed, calm and at peace with myself could possibly dump me on the ground so hard.

With such a ready source available, our appetite for hash grew out of all proportion, and pretty soon we were stoned almost round the clock. It was all I could do to manage to hold my head together on everyday matters, like serving behind the bar and giving people the right change – if I knew there wasn't a chance I could rip them off. It transpired that Harvey and his travelling companion – who had moved on in search of more adventures after just a short time at the Bluesy – had been trying to peddle their slabs along the way, but with little success. Switzerland didn't take kindly to drugs, hard or soft, so they'd not been able to make many inroads.

After a few weeks, we decided to move on. I handed in my notice, hung up my working clothes for the last

time, and joined Harvey for an overland trek through
Europe. With all the money I'd earned and stolen
during my time at the hotel we were well provided for,
and passed an enjoyable couple of months staying at
youth hostels, eating and drinking well, smoking dope –
and all the time talking about this increasingly urgent
need to 'find yourself'.

We went to Athens, Corfu and finally Crete, where we
rented some rooms and moved in with a couple of girls
we met at one of the harbour bars. With the money I'd
amassed we bought in crates of beer every day. Life was
one long party. Finally May arrived, though, and the
starting date for my second summer season at the Crazy
Horse Saloon. Harvey and I had our last drinks together
and waved each other a cheery goodbye – each to
continue our own search for something we weren't quite
sure of. I sometimes wonder whether he's still looking.

Back at Santa Suzanna it was more of the same from
the previous year. All-night partying in the bar, musical
beds with the girls hanging around after closing time,
and late mornings spent trying to recover from the
previous night's activities.

Yet somehow I seemed to be losing my taste for it all.
It was like a bottle of lemonade that had gone flat
because the top had been left off. All the ingredients
were still there, but it had no fizz. I actually found
myself on occasions dreading the prospect of having to
go through the motions of passion with another sun-
burned, vodka-fuelled 'holiday fling' seeker. Even the
fighting spirit in me was ebbing away. Partly this was
because of my increasingly heavy drug use, which slowed
my emotions down, but it also reflected this growing
sense I had that I was missing out on something more
meaningful, somewhere. Now and then I'd try to talk
about it with the other lads at the bar, but they'd laugh it
off.

'Say, do you ever wonder what it's all about – life, I
mean?' I'd ask casually over a breakfast beer, perhaps.

'What d'ya mean, Johnny? It's women and drinking, isn't it? What more could you want, eh?'

Or someone else would chip in: 'Not thinking of becoming a monk, are you Johnny? Just because you didn't score last night!' And my questions would be drowned in a sea of guffaws, giggles and empty ale-can missiles.

But I couldn't shake my inner restlessness. I worried away at it even while I was at my busiest taking orders, running round with trays full of drinks, and strong-arming those revellers who had had one too many out of the door. I'd watch the young holidaymakers come in, dressed up in their evening best. They'd drink more than they should, stagger away in the early hours laughing and hooting. It all seemed more and more empty to me. 'Surely there's got to be more to life than working in some dead-end job fifty weeks of a year so that you can come and get a hangover in the sun?' I'd ask myself.

Eventually I became so unsettled that I knew I had to do something. One day I hurriedly quit my job to see if I could find some answers to the questions Harvey had prompted me to start asking.

Finding my way to Marrakesh, a hot and dusty city in Morocco, I booked into a cheap hotel and began to hang around in the bars and hostels where young intense travellers from all over Europe seemed to gather to share their drugs and their hunger for reality. Some days I'd consume more than even my hash-saturated system could take, and I'd be unable to do more than lie on my bed staring up at the cracked ceiling, listening to the flies buzzing around and the shouts from the street below, half hoping that someone would arrive at my door to tell me what on earth was going on.

Then I began to get hit by deep troughs of depression. Great, black clouds of gloom would overwhelm me. I'd feel pressed to the spot by foreboding of some uncertain but huge catastrophe. Eating and washing seemed completely unimportant. I became suspicious of the other travellers, thinking that they were out to steal my money or my dope. Everywhere I went I'd be constantly turning my head to see if someone was trying to sneak up behind me.

Such paranoia finally spurred me to leave Morocco, and I found my way to Gibraltar. Funds were low by now, so I managed to find a few days' work bricklaying at a new hotel complex. I also went into an expensive shop and bought a couple of cameras and a cassette player on HP. I left the country a couple of days later.

Soon I was back at the Crazy Horse Saloon, anxious to tell the other guys about my travels and experiences. I stayed on for a couple of weeks, but the job no longer held any appeal. From there I moved on to Lorette, where I shared an apartment with Fanta, whom I had met through the saloon. He shared my appetite for hash, and we began to push it in the town as well as taking huge quantities ourselves.

When the season ended and it was time to head back to Nottingham once more, I was little more than skin and bone, withdrawn and suspicious of everyone around me. Large, raw ulcers in my mouth meant that on the few occasions I felt like eating, I couldn't because it was too painful. My lips were sore and cracked, and I was plagued by stomach cramps.

Somehow I managed to stumble back to my parents' house, where the full extent of my physical slump hit me. When Mum opened the door, she didn't recognise me.

By now I was beyond holding a job down. I made one or two attempts to resume bricklaying, but the demands of timekeeping and the physical hardship were too much for me. More often than not I'd simply lie in late in the mornings, and then manage to shuffle down to the local pub to drink away the afternoons.

I managed to make enough contacts to feed my drug craving, but didn't feel free to smoke at home. So I moved out, into a dirty one-room flat a couple of streets away. There was a bed with a few dirty covers, a tatty old wardrobe, a broken-down chair and a sink. As well as making me more docile, the drugs reduced my sex drive. And I then found that on the nights I did go out looking for some female company, my unkempt, un-shaven, unwashed appearance kept them away.

So it was one morning that I hung over the sink in my damp attic room, and looked up at the mirror. As I examined my face – old before its time – I remembered that time hovering over the industrial chimney, the dark drop in front of me, and thought how similar the situation was now.

'You're falling apart, Johnny,' I told myself. 'You're really on the edge, you know, youth. If you aren't careful, you're going to fall into the flames.'

What worried me most was that the face I was gazing into didn't seem to care.

7

The Silent Scream

I was flying off to start a brand new life – so I got drunk to celebrate. Together with a gang of other bricklayers, I'd boarded the plane taking off from London's Heathrow, looking forward to the prospect of a bright new future in Canada.

The realisation that I was literally wasting away had hit me hard that day in my shabby flat. I'd not been able to shake the sense of alarm it had provoked, which had remained with me as things went from bad to worse. With every spare penny going on drink and drugs I'd fallen well behind on rent payments. When I knew the landlord was coming – I could hear the barking of his two fierce dogs well down the street – I'd turn off the stereo and the lights and lie quietly on my bed, waiting for him to give up knocking and go away. I'd hear him curse and kick the wall as he stamped off.

One day he'd caught me leaving, though, and told me bluntly: 'I want you out, Goodfellow. You owe me money and you're nothing but trouble. You've got to get out.'

My parents had let me move back into my old room. If they were worried for me, they were not prepared to say anything. But moving home again prompted me to try working again, so I found myself back on the building sites for a short time. During one lunchtime break in the snack cabin, I casually picked up a lunchtime edition of the evening paper that had been tossed aside by one of the other men. He'd seen that there were no fanciable runners on the afternoon's race card and decided there were no bets worth placing.

I flipped the pages idly, until I came to the advertisement section. As I looked down the columns, one entry seemed to leap out at me. 'Canada. Top rates for bricklayers. Free flights, good money. Apply now for further information.' I read on, drinking in the details about the money that was waiting to be earned working in the beautiful Canadian countryside. It sounded wonderful – and a welcome relief from the cold, wet monotony of the Midlands.

Perhaps this was what I needed, I thought. A new place. New friends. New prospects. A chance to break with the past and build a new future. I'd been able to discipline myself to work hard in the past, and here was an opportunity to do so once more. I could do it. I could pull myself together if I really tried, and save myself from complete collapse. All it needed was a bit of determination, effort and willpower. I read the advert aloud to the men sitting around and one or two expressed mild curiosity. I then carefully tore it out of the page and slipped it into my pocket.

Within ten days I was in Canada. I'd telephoned the number listed in the advertisement and had been invited down to Birmingham for an interview. After being accepted there I'd simply had to wait for all my paperwork to be processed before I joined the other brickies – including two of my Nottingham workmates – at Heathrow. Three times the salary of Britain, good fresh air and fine living – we toasted each other's good fortune from take-off to touchdown. I saw this airborne party as a sort of suitable farewell to my old life. I was determined to make a go of things in the days to come.

And I did. We had been contracted to work on a major apartment complex in St John, New Brunswick, on Canada's eastern seaboard. Local labourers didn't like the harsh winters and managed to make enough money during the summer months – hence the appeal for British hands to keep the bricks being laid. For the first week we were accommodated at a comfortable hotel in the town, after which we were expected to find our own accommodation. I got myself a smart bedsitting room in a lodging house not far from the site. It was clean, cosy and convenient, and I soon felt as though I'd found myself a new home.

The work was hard, but with my determination to make a new start I responded willingly. We would find that it was so cold on some mornings that big heater fans would be set blowing on each level of the building to keep the freshly-mixed mortar from freezing and cracking before we could use it. Some days it was twenty-five degrees below freezing. But though it was colder than Nottingham, it was cleaner, too, and I enjoyed breathing in the crisp morning air.

I resolved from the word go to keep my head down and work hard. I wanted to make as much money as soon as possible. I was looking for a home, a wife and a family – and I figured that by pulling myself together and really trying, I'd be able to make it all happen. So I disciplined myself hard. No drugs, no crazy nights, no heavy drinking.

At the end of the day I was normally fairly tired because my body was still getting back into the swing of hard labour. I'd go back to my room, weary but satisfied, wash and change and then head down the street to a nearby bar. There I would enjoy a leisurely meal of medium steak and plenty of vegetables, followed by no more than four or five quiet pints with a few of the other regulars (just a sip compared to my former intake). Then I'd stroll back to my lodgings and climb into bed for a contented night's sleep, satisfied with my efforts of the day and the prospects of tomorrow.

This ordered pattern continued for a week or so, until one Friday night. As I was heading along the corridor to my room, I accidentally collided with someone walking in the opposite direction. He was a tall, broad, bearded French Canadian who had moved into the adjoining room. As we stepped away from each other and looked up, I mumbled an apology.

He looked at me for a moment and then asked matter-of-factly: 'Do you smoke dope?'

'Sure I do,' I answered quickly and eagerly, as a part of me seemed to stand back and look on in horror as all my resolutions and plans seemed to be swept away in an instant. Even as we turned to head back to his room I was appalled at the way in which all my efforts seemed about to crumble to nothing. But this feeling was swamped by an overwhelming desire to feel the wonderful rush of floating freedom that hit me as I sucked in the joint. As we closed the door, I hoped it was good stuff.

It was, and abstinence seemed to add to the pleasure. Frankie and I sat down and swapped hash stories as he took his from its hiding place, burned it over some silver paper, and then rolled it into two large joints. The familiar, pungent sweetness made me wrinkle my nose as I drew heavily on my smoke.

We spent several hours getting thoroughly stoned before we went out on the town. In a series of bars and discos I managed to spend most of the money I'd earned during my brief time in Canada. We returned to our rooms with empty pockets, but each with a woman on our arm. They stayed the night, and we alternately slept and smoked through till dawn. The next day was a Saturday, but with us working a six- or seven-day week we were due in on site.

I didn't go. Instead the four of us stayed in our rooms, smoking and drinking through the weekend. I woke on Tuesday morning feeling hung over, heavy-headed ... and defeated. All the pleasure of the past few days seemed to drain away as I realised that my best efforts had come to nothing. I was back where I had started, and there didn't seem to be anything I could do about it.

So began an ongoing struggle, as I'd try to make sure I arrived in time for work every morning and continued to enjoy the wild living at night again. Some nights we would be out dancing and drinking until 3 am, returning for a couple of hours of unrefreshing sleep before getting up again at 6.30 am. Soon I was skipping more than the odd day again, and I was turning up only two or three mornings a week – putting in just enough hours to cover the costs of accommodation, drink and drugs.

I couldn't bring myself to tell any of this to my family back home. My first letters on arrival had been enthusiastic and cheerful. I'd told them how exciting Canada was, and how well things were going. As I slipped back into my old ways, I began to make my notes briefer and less frequent, until eventually I stopped writing at all. Except for one note – to tell them I was getting married.

I'd met Corinne in a disco one night, and I'd been attracted to her immediately. She was a beautiful French Canadian with an oval face, dark brown eyes and long, dark hair. I got talking to her over a drink and so began a relationship that blossomed in the days that followed.

Although fairly quiet by nature, she enjoyed the excitement of nightlife, too, and after an evening's drinking in bars and clubs we would head off back to my apartment with a bottle of whisky and some hash. Within a few weeks I had proposed and she had accepted. We intended to get married in a matter of months and set up home together. Corinne made me happy and lessened the disappointment I'd felt over failing to make a clean break. Here was someone who shared my love for the buzz of drugs and drinking, and simply helped me keep it all under some sort of control. Maybe it was possible to tread a middle line, after all.

I told myself that Corinne made me feel different from the way all the other girls had made me feel. There had been plenty of other women, but they had been objects, not people. I'd never felt comfortable talking to them, thinking of them as people with needs and feelings and hurts. I'd just been interested in whether or not they'd go to bed with me, and how I could drop them afterwards without a scene. It was partly a horrible sense of awkwardness and also a deep insecurity. I'd never got used to that awful moment when you had to go up and ask a girl if she wanted to dance. I dreaded the moment when she may say 'no', and the feelings of rejection and ridicule you'd experience in front of your mates. So I'd kept them at arm's length, except in bed, and continued to be baffled by the way I desperately wanted to pursue them, but didn't seem able to get close once I'd caught them. The threat of true intimacy frightened me.

It had seemed otherwise for a time with Sharon. At eighteen I'd met her in a Nottingham club, a slim, blonde-haired secretary from a respectable, middle-class home. It was before I'd really started to go wild, and we began a courtship that seemed stable and contented. One day she looked ashen as we met after work, and she blurted out: 'Johnny, you'll never believe it: I'm pregnant!'

The shock threw us together. We were terrified at what our parents would say, but there seemed to be no way out. We faced two sets of silent, saddened parents as we told them what had happened, and began to plan for the future. Initially we intended to get married, but as the plans became more serious I began to panic. With little thought for Sharon and our baby, all I could see was my freedom being taken away; a young man with all his future ahead of him stuck at home with a wife, a child and too many responsibilities. The prospect alarmed me, and in an emotional scene I had told her it was all off; then I'd turned around, walked out of her life and concentrated on my own. If I remember rightly, the first thing I did was to go and have a few drinks.

Memories of this failed relationship began to come back to me as Corinne and I found that we weren't going to be following a smooth path to the altar. Although at first being with her had curbed my excessive appetite for drugs, gradually her presence began to act as less of a brake. I would get heavily stoned, or drink myself almost to a standstill, and we would fall out about it. The way I pushed the limits of what I could handle seemed to frighten her, despite her own love of getting high.

Things came to a head one night when we swayed back to my new room. Erratic work schedules had slimmed my pay packets down drastically, and as a result I'd had to move from the comfortable lodgings I'd had previously to less tasteful accommodation in a poorer part of the town.

I collapse back on the bed and stare up at the bare electric bulb swinging from the ceiling. The light burns into the back of my eyes, but the sharp stabbing pain it causes is a welcome attack on the spreading numbness I feel across my chest and stomach.

I can hear Corinne's footsteps fading down the corridor as she leaves. I know that I'm never going to see her again, that the cottage with the roses round the door and the smiling kids aren't going to be. She's just slammed the door shut and walked out in despair, and I'm not sure what to feel. It's a bit like being awake under anaesthetic. I'm conscious of my body and the reality of what's just happened, but I seem to be beyond feeling anything. The last flicker of hope I had about this quest for a new life has been snuffed out and I seem to be beyond reacting.

Water drips maddeningly into the cracked, brown-stained washbasin in the corner of the room, and around my ankles I can sense the drift of cool air that whispers in between the cracks in the uncovered, wooden floorboards. Unmoving, I look at the ceiling and run my tongue, thick with alcohol, over my lips. A thought crosses my mind, definite and direct.

I've completely lost control of my life.

At first it's just a fact, unavoidable and inarguable. But

then it seems to become a lockgate that opens, allowing floods of emotion to come crashing through. A wave of cold, sharp fear surges through me as I try to look into the future and realise that there is nothing there to see, not the faintest straw of a hope to clutch at. I feel like I'm drowning in the sea of my own failure.

Each new realisation beats down upon me like another wave crashing against a harbour wall. No one knows that I'm lying in this filthy room all alone. I have no friends to whom I can turn for help. My drinking is out of any control. I can't seem to get enough drugs to satisfy my cravings. It's beyond me to show care and concern for someone I love dearly. Tomorrow seems like a big, black hole. It's like being on the chimneytop again.

I've heard about dying men who are supposed to see a film of their life flash before their eyes. Well, my time must be near, because I'm staring at a private screening of John Goodfellow's life – a series of explosive, empty adventures. I'm appalled, overwhelmed and terrified. I can't move from the top of this broken-down old brass bed.

Suddenly I jerk forward from the waist as, in an agonising wrench, a huge silent scream bursts from my lips. No sound comes out, but my teeth are bared and my mouth pulled wide as I shriek inwardly in horror. It's like vomiting despair.

Falling back onto the bedspread again, I close my eyes to try to stop the stinging sensation in my eyes. As I drift into a welcome alcoholic sleep I half hope that I won't wake up in the morning because I don't think I'll be able to face the thought of another day in my pointless, hopeless life.

Cold, cramped and hung over, I came round the next morning with the awareness that something strange and frightening had happened a few hours earlier. It wasn't just the drugs and drink, there had been something else clawing at my heart. But I was in no mood for working it out. I simply knew that I had to get out of that room and to leave Canada as soon as I could.

The final reason for staying there had fallen through, together with my hopes for a new, self-made start. And with Corinne out of my life, the possibilities of my staying in Canada had gone whether I wanted to remain or not. A couple of months earlier there had been an early morning visit to the building site by a couple of officials from the Canadian government.

They turned out to be men from the immigration department, and their investigations had revealed that a number of British bricklayers – including me – had made false declarations to get the necessary papers to allow them into the country. What I'd done was fail to admit to my criminal conviction for the jeweller's shop break-in. Now they'd found out and wanted me out of Canada. My engagement to Corrine had worked a rescue, though, because anyone marrying a Canadian citizen automatically won the relevant authorisation to stay. Now with my ring off her finger, my papers would soon come to the top of the immigration department's in-tray again.

If I'd felt threatened like this only a few weeks before, I would have responded with a flash of the violent Johnny of old. It had happened once, despite my best intentions to keep a tight rein on my temper and fists, one night after I'd been out for a few drinks with Frankie. We were strolling home with a couple of girls when we passed two other guys in the street. One of them, a tall, long-haired man in a lumber jacket, brushed my shoulder awkwardly. Instinctively I swore a warning at him to be more careful in future.

Provoked, he turned back and we were soon trading blows in the middle of the street. I was beginning to work him over well when his buddy stepped back from struggling with Frankie and reached into his inside pocket, pulling out a wicked-looking bowie knife and brandishing it at us with a grin.

Our rooms weren't far away, so I turned and ran inside. Grabbing a knife from the kitchen, I charged back into the street to confront them, screaming and yelling like a maniac.

For a few moments we stood off from each other. I was just waiting for them to make a move, and I'd dive at them with my blade. But after flashing us a last look of anger, they turned and walked away.

But now all the fight seemed to have gone out of me. It wasn't that I was peaceful and controlled inside. I was just beaten; whipped like a dog. I felt as though I'd been attacked by a gang and left for dead at the side of the road. I just wanted to crawl into a quiet place where I could wait for the end.

The morning after Corinne's departure, I knew I had to leave. I booked a ticket back to England with the little money I had saved, and the next day boarded a flight home. Stepping down onto the tarmac at Heathrow I didn't dare look further than getting through customs. If there was any point or hope, then all I knew was that it was beyond me. I shuffled in line to the exit that seemed to mock my despair: 'Nothing to Declare'.

8

Beyond Reality

No one ever asked me what had happened to the plans for a bright new life. They didn't have to: one look at me told the whole story of failure. I was thin and sickly, and any shred of confidence I may have once possessed had been stripped away by my experiences in Canada. I was cowed and quiet, and tried to avoid talking with people at all times because I just couldn't cope with attempting to communicate.

Being at home was dreadful, so I'd slope off down to one of the pubs, where I'd buy a pint and sit, withdrawn, in a corner or up against the bar. I'd sip my beer, look around at all the people laughing and joking, and all the feelings of being separated – like I was stuck on the other side of a one-way mirror – would come back at me, magnified. Life was just a mechanical round of finally dragging myself out of bed, shuffling through the day until the bars were open, drinking silently until it was time to go home, falling into bed and waiting for the whole meaningless routine to start again.

Then, one night, I bumped into Alan. I was nursing a drink in a corner of the Flying Horse. I was watching the chatter and drinking going on around me in a detached sort of way when I spotted someone I thought I recognised from school days. We got talking as he waited to be served, and it turned out to be Alan, whom I used to know. But he'd changed.

Back at school, when I'd been recognised as one of the

leading lights – because of my temper and talent for fighting – he'd been quiet. Tall, thin and spotty, he'd been just another one of the boys. Now here was I, introspective and unsure of myself and everything else, and Alan seemed to have made an opposite transformation.

Wearing a smart leather jacket he seemed confident and self-assured. Buying me a pint with a gesture of casual generosity, he mentioned that he had a sports car parked just outside. I got the impression that he was really doing well for himself, although he was faintly vague about what he did for a living. Whatever it was, it certainly seemed to be successful enough. Somehow we struck up an immediate friendship, recalling the old days and wondering what had happened to some of the other boys we had known. By the end of the evening we'd agreed to meet up again the following night to go and score some dope together.

Over the next few weeks, Alan and I became close friends. We'd drink until closing time and then go back to his flat in another part of the town, where we'd smoke dope until we nodded off in the small hours. Early on I discovered that Alan's successful appearance was only that. He was out of work and the TR7 was on hire purchase, with a few payments outstanding. I sensed that, in his own way, Alan felt as empty inside as I did.

One evening as we sat drowsily in his cheap flat, drawing on a joint and talking with the lazy sort of contentment that only dope can give, Alan broke the conversation and asked me unexpectedly: 'Do you ever think about spiritual things, then, Johnny?'

I squinted at him through the smoke, furrowing my eyebrows in a question. 'Eh? Spiritual things? I don't know what you mean.'

'Well, you know, life. Don't you ever wonder what life's all about, like – why we are here and all? You know, the future and death and everything?'

My heart had started to race as he began to talk, but

somehow I didn't dare admit to having shared such thoughts. I was frightened about opening up, about exposing what was really inside me – the horrible feeling of emptiness, loneliness and uncertainty. So I responded in a non-committal way: 'No, I can't say I've thought about that sort of stuff in years.' But I didn't want him to stop talking, so I added: 'Why d'you ask, Alan?'

He got up quickly and walked over to a wall cupboard. Rummaging about in the back, he pulled out a large, black book and walked back. Sitting down next to me on the sofa, he dropped the book onto the coffee table in front of us.

'Well, I was wondering whether you were interested in any of this,' he said, pointing to the book. I looked down at the cover.

Hidden and Forbidden Knowledge it proclaimed in large gold letters.

I picked the book up to have a flip through it, as I could sense that Alan was trying to share his excitement with me about something. Skipping through the thick volume, I saw photographs and articles about all sorts of occult phenomena and experiences. There were features and studies on tarot cards, astrology, astral projection, clairvoyance, clairaudience and black magic. There were guidelines for magic rites and drawing pentagrams and other symbols.

The book seemed to grow heavier in my hands. Here was what I'd been looking for! Maybe there were answers to some of the questions I'd been asking myself, after all! I pored over the pages, thrilled by this whole new world that was being unveiled before my eyes, with all its possibilities for meaning and purpose. Maybe this was the missing piece that I'd been searching for, I thought excitedly.

When I finally left Alan's flat later that night, I had *Hidden and Forbidden Knowledge* tucked under my arm.

For the next fortnight I spent almost every waking moment with my nose stuck in its pages, drawn to reading, rereading and studying it with a strange compulsion. I didn't understand all that was said, but I sensed, reading between the lines, that it was hugely important. My whole life was at stake, and this could be the answer.

From then on Alan and I talked about nothing else. We'd read sections of the book together and discuss what various aspects meant and how they might be applied to our lives. We became particularly drawn to astrology and the idea that our lives might in some way be influenced by the alignment of the planets and the stars.

This possibility both attracted and repelled me. I was filled with hope by the idea that all those times I'd spun out of control – violence, drugs and sex – may have been beyond my governing. But I was also consumed by dread at the prospect that what happened in the heavens was charting my future. There may be worse things ahead.

Every day I'd read what the newspaper astrologers had to say for Aquarius, but I soon began to dismiss these columns as trivial. Through visiting occult bookshops and buying up more literature, Alan and I began to realise that there was a far deeper side to this whole new world that we had discovered than most people were aware of.

Alan's pretty blonde girlfriend, Sarah, shared a flat with another girl, Jenny, and the four of us would spend long evenings talking about the things we were reading. Alan and I began to try to make objects move by psychokinesis, and there were occasions when I really believed that the mug on the table in front of me was shimmering and vibrating because of the power we were releasing from within.

We also became fascinated by what we read of astral projection. These were mystical out-of-the-body experiences that people apparently had after going into a trance. Their inner being, or spirit, would be freed from their physical body and they would be able to travel to different places and dimensions, and learn new and secret truths about life. Despite fuelling our efforts with larger and larger quantities of dope, Alan and I were frustrated by our failure to travel on these incredible journeys.

The girls were more successful, though – and it frightened them. One evening Sarah told us how the previous night she had found herself leaving her body as she was drawn into the astral plane. Suddenly she found herself in front of the bathroom mirror – but there was a different face staring out at her. Then she turned and looked back into the bedroom ... and saw her own body lying in bed. The experience had shocked her deeply, and she never tried to go 'visiting' again in this way. Alan and I were excited by her account, though, and it only added to our sense of annoyance that we had not managed to achieve similar things.

We felt that we were very close to something; quite what we didn't really know, but it was a matter of life or death.

It's like we've been let in on a secret that's too big for the rest of the world. We watch all the people heading off for work in the morning with their briefcases, sandwich boxes and umbrellas, and they look at us as though we're ordinary, just like them. But they don't know. We're on the edge of something so important that only a few people can be trusted with it.

All the things you see around you – houses, cars, children playing in the park – are what most people think are 'real'. If only they knew! We're being shown that in a crazy way everything around us is unreal and that there is a greater reality just a hair's breadth away. It's so tantalisingly close, but it's also just out of reach.

There are keys, you see. Keys to understanding and power that will unlock the universe. They are so important that they are not to be made known to ordinary people – only those with a hunger for more.

Alan and I are part of a small calling who have been chosen to have these truths revealed to us. Some of the others have formed groups that contain secret messages in the music they weave. To us the likes of Hawkwind, Pink Floyd and Jethro Tull are musical prophets, speaking of deep things. We spend hours searching every phrase and tone, looking for the coded words.

It's thrilling and terrifying, both at the same time. I feel as though I could either fall off this planet and go spinning helplessly into deepest space, never to return, or find myself being crowned as a king of the entire universe. Life and death; they dance together inside me, spinning faster and faster. The music is going to stop soon, and one of the partners is going to have to bow to the other. I wonder which one it's going to be.

Our search became so obsessive that we never spoke about anything else. While we felt that we had been chosen especially to learn about these hidden landscapes of life, we also felt a responsibility to share some of this teaching with others.

We tried to explain to drinking partners in the pubs and clubs how the world was on the brink of a series of cataclysmic events, and that people had to find the keys that would unlock the past, the present and the future. We weren't put off by their looks of blank incomprehension, nor the nickname we quickly earned as 'The Prophets of Doom'. We knew, deep inside, that our quest was too important to be put off by people's lack of understanding.

Alan suggested that one way we could be helped in our search would be to seek guidance from the country's top astrologer. We had read all his bestselling books on the subject. Perhaps if we showed him our commitment to finding the truth, he would be able to help. We discovered that he organised a weekly meeting in London to discuss astrological issues, and we excitedly travelled down one Wednesday to the lodge where the group met.

It was a crushing disappointment. We'd been expecting to find a man of hypnotic attraction, a leader. Instead he turned out to be a rather nondescript, quiet little man who couldn't even look us in the eyes when we introduced ourselves. And the other members of the group – who we'd anticipated would be like an inner circle of wise devotees – seemed to us just a group of middle-aged, middle-class surburbanites with a passing fancy for astrology.

We stayed for the meeting, and an elderly man with big, bushy eyebrows babbled on about some obscure aspect of astrology. We left in despair. Our high hopes had been dashed. We felt cheated and yet at the same time agreed that while they had only been playing at it, our exploration of the meaning of life was deadly serious.

In some ways the disappointment only sharpened our desire to find the truth, and we spent more and more time locked in study, trying to fall into trances and searching acid rock music for messages and guidance.

Our search consumed our nights and days. We'd sit up until the early hours, when a restless kind of sleep finally overtook us. By now I was working as a self-employed bricklayer, so if I didn't feel like going in the next morning, I wouldn't. The money I earned as a sub-contractor when I was working made up for the days I missed. When I stayed at home, Alan and I would meet over lunch to talk about our thoughts and studies, then go down the pub and drink and talk until afternoon closing time. From there we would head back either to Alan's place or mine (I'd moved out of home again, to my family's combined relief and concern, and found a shabby room to let in the building where Sarah and

Jenny shared) and smoke some more dope. That would keep us going until evening, when there would be another round of drinking and dope and talk about 'the keys'.

We were joined in our erratic work arrangement by a group of other self-employed brickies, who included Mac. Big, broad, with sharp features, Mac loved to drink and womanise, and was always in the thick of the fun. (I'd known him from my time in Spain and Canada.) Yet when he heard Alan and me talking about our search, he didn't just laugh it off and disappear for another drink. He began to ask questions about what we were doing, and gradually joined our nightly sessions of study, drink and dope. With him came Gary, whom we also knew from the local drinking scene.

Shorter than Mac, with a mass of thick curly black hair, he had been married, but was separated from his wife. He always seemed to have plenty of money, but no one was ever quite sure where it all came from. And it was best not to ask.

Between us, we four had sampled just about every-thing life had to offer a young man. And yet as we sat together, drinking and talking and smoking and talking, we all agreed that for every slice of action we'd known, there was still an emptiness inside. We were only in our early and mid-twenties, yet in some ways we felt like old men with nothing to look forward to. Only this prospect of there being something else, something outside our-selves, held any hope or sense.

One night we were all squeezed into my dirty room, finishing off a couple of joints, when I suddenly felt as though the clouds in my head had parted, and I could see the way ahead clearly.

'You know, lads, we've got to find God.'

They looked over at me and waited for me to continue.

'Look, we all know that there's more to life than what people see out there' – and I pointed to the street below – 'right? Well, then, there must be some kind of supreme power or being who's in control of the universe, right? And if we can find him, then he – or it, or whatever – will be able to help us understand ourselves; show us all the mysteries we're searching for.'

Alan agreed: 'Yeah ... that's right, Johnny. We all believe that there is some supreme being out there. So it must be able to be found – and when we do, we'll find the answers.'

We all started to grin and nod to each other. There was a thrill of excitement as we felt that we'd really hit on something important. We all crammed into Alan's car and drove down into the town, where we went to Frodo's, a noisy cellar wine bar, to celebrate.

We got well and truly drunk that night, and when people around asked what the toasts were about, we grinned and told them: 'We're going to go and find God!'

The sense of euphoria carried us over the next few days, and we began to discuss how we might start to search for God. We talked about it and agreed that we should begin by seeking help from holy men who might be able to put us on the right track. The church never entered our thinking at this stage. We'd all had similar experiences of a sterile faith that mouthed love and mocked sincerity, and we dismissed Christianity as being as empty as the collection plates that we'd all passed along the pew in our younger days.

Up to now the people in our drinking circles had humoured our talk about the supernatural world, but with our pubtime planning sessions for the search for God, some began to get more concerned.

'Don't you think you're all taking this a bit too far, lads, eh?' they would ask from time to time. A few even dared to catch one of the others when they were alone and cautiously suggest that maybe Johnny really needed to see a doctor.

When I read in a library book about a band of mystics who lived in the remote mountains of Iran, deeply spiritual nomads who performed ancient rites in their communion with the gods, I knew that I had found the route we needed to follow. I filled the others in about these horse-riding gurus, and said: 'These are the men. These are the ones who can help us find God. We've got to go and find them.'

It quickly became clear, on pooling our limited assets, that we didn't have the money we needed to fund such a trip. My fear of the future spurred me into action. I had to explore this hazy world of spiritual things, yet I was frightened to do so alone. By enthusing the others, I could persuade them to join me. With my desperate passion for meaning driving me, I took on the role of ringleader, and began to scheme of ways to get us on the road to the Middle East. After a few late nights, I had it, and I called a council of war to lay the plan before the others.

I told them that we needed some initial money, so we all had to pull a fraud to get some easy cash. I'd carried out a couple of similar rip-offs in the past and knew that it was relatively quick and easy to get money this way; there would be no problem. With the money we made, we would then have to buy a van and travel overland. If we ran short along the way, it would be easy enough for the four of us to find a victim of some sorts to provide some more money.

Alan, Mac and Gary nodded in agreement. 'Sounds good, Johnny. But where do we get all this together?'

I didn't hesitate in replying, although I don't think I knew what was going to tumble out of my lips as I opened my mouth.

'Amsterdam. We're going to go to Amsterdam and start from there.'

As I said it, I knew that it was right – but I didn't know why. I'd only been to Amsterdam once before, and it had been an experience I had been glad to leave behind as quickly as possible.

It had been during my weeks travelling in search of

'the scene' that Harvey had introduced me to. I'd heard so much about Amsterdam. It was like the fountainhead of the drug trail that wound its way from Europe down through into the Middle East and beyond. All kinds of drugs were sold openly on the streets. Some cafes even had little marijuana leaf signs on the windows, and you were able to buy a couple of sticks over the counter, or baked into a cake. You just had to go to experience it, I was told; it was so free and easy, so laid back, so beautiful.

When I arrived at the city's Central Station, my pockets were still bulging from the proceeds of my time at the Crazy Horse Saloon. Yet a crippling sense of fear gripped me almost as soon as I stepped out of the cavernous railway station. There were smiling, dope-hazed faces all around me; young jean-clad groups clustered around guitars on street corners; and graffiti urging 'love not war' everywhere – but I felt completely ill at ease.

I completed a quick walking tour of the city, and then headed off down into one of the large parks that ring the centre. Although I was carrying enough to pay for a suite of rooms at any of Amsterdam's plushest hotels, I was too scared to set foot inside. Instead, I spent a nervous night sleeping curled up on a park bench, and the next morning I took the first train out.

Memories of this unsettling visit came back to me, but I still knew for some inexplicable reason that Amsterdam was the place from which we should set off in our search for God.

There was an awkward kind of farewell at home when I went round to my parents and sisters to explain, vaguely, that I and a group of friends were 'going off travelling for a while'. I'd told them a little about my fascination with supernatural things, but they'd shown no interest, and I didn't want to have to try explaining now. As I left, Trish said to Mum in a matter-of-fact voice: 'I don't think I'm going to see Johnny again.'

In a curious way, she was right.

When I met up with Alan, Mac and Gary at East Midlands Airport, and we boarded the plane, we were charged up at the thought of starting our pilgrimage. 'Amsterdam, here we come,' I thought, as we were sucked back into our seats by the take-off thrust.

I didn't realise what a crossroads it would turn out to be.

9

Caught at the Crossroads

The Shelter was like a cross between an army barracks and a hospital. There was an air of cleanliness, orderliness and drilled routine about the three-storey building tucked away in one of the side streets in the rougher quarter of Amsterdam's city centre. The crisp well-run friendliness of the place both attracted us and repelled us as we set our bags down at the side of our bunk beds.

We'd been guided here by the people we'd asked on the streets about the best place to stay. 'The Shelter – cleanest and cheapest in the city,' they'd all said. So we'd wound our way through the narrow, cobbled streets; across arched bridges over the tree-lined canals, until we'd found the place, where a small sign at the side of the door announced that it was a 'Christian youth hostel'.

This short walk from the Central Station, where we'd been dropped by the airport bus, had taken us into the very heart of Amsterdam's street scene. On the way we'd passed crowds of young people milling around like a flowing stream of colour with their bright clothes and bags. But we'd also noticed those at the side of the roadways who, by comparison, seemed to have been washed up like so much floating rubbish. Heroin addiction screamed from their dark, grey-ringed eyes, emaciated bodies and unkempt clothing.

In all my desperate days I had never touched heroin because the prospect of what it could do had terrified me. Yet as I passed so many wasted youngsters, lying or crouching every few yards it seemed, I felt as though I was being warned about just where I was headed if this pilgrimage didn't work out. The thought scared me, and I took a tighter grip on my suitcase, increased my pace, and urged the other three to get a move on.

From the crowds and pushers and users we passed into the centre of the city's red light district, famed the world over for its easy-going and permissive nature. Anything and everything went in Amsterdam, they said. Whatever your sexual inclinations, there would be someone prepared to indulge you if you could pay the price, or somewhere you could watch others if that was your thing. We walked down the canal-side streets where the prostitutes sat in small, red-lit windows, wearing little or nothing and urging the passing men to step inside, draw the curtains and hand over the notes.

In days gone by this broad-minded, bold display of liberation would have been heady stuff. I'd have responded like a little boy let loose in a sweet shop. But by now my only thought was our goal; we had to find God! So I scarcely did more than turn my head to one side occasionally to cast a faintly-curious eye over the surroundings as we tramped along the directions we'd been given to The Shelter.

Up on the first floor of The Shelter we were ushered into a large dormitory which was filled with two rows of bunks, enough to accommodate about forty people. Picking our beds, testing the mattresses, we claimed our sleeping pitches, and then transferred our belongings to the lockers at the other end of the room. We then went to explore the rest of the building and found wooden floors and green-tiled walls decorated with posters and paintings proclaiming love and peace. There were a lot of other young travellers like us around, and yet there was an almost unnaturally subdued atmosphere, rather like the reading room of a library.

Next morning, after a good night's sleep, we breakfasted and pulled up stools together in the refectory area downstairs. Huddled forwards with elbows on the tables over mugs of steaming coffee, we ran through the plan again in low voices, casting an eye over our shoulders from time to time to make sure that no one was eavesdropping.

Simplicity was the key. The art of good fraud was keeping it uncluttered; the less fanciful the tale you spun, the less likely people were to quiz you about it. My earlier criminal exploits had already proved that, and I'd successfully completed one swindle back in England. I'd travelled down to London by train and on arriving at Euston pretended that I'd lost all my luggage. Returning to Nottingham – with the 'crime' suitably reported to the Metropolitan Police – I'd claimed on my previously-arranged holiday insurance for the loss of my luggage, clothing and expensive new cassette player. It was a profitable day's outing, really – none of those things had actually existed.

This was the crime we intended to commit to finance our overland trip to the East. We'd all taken out holiday insurances prior to leaving Nottingham, making sure that we used different companies so that we wouldn't arouse any suspicion. From our Amsterdam base, we intended to go four separate ways – Alan to Belgium, Gary to Germany and Mac to France – and report luggage thefts in four different locations. Then we'd meet back in Amsterdam, claim the money and be on our way.

My restlessness spurred me into going first; I also wanted to show the others how easy it was. Driven, too, by a continuing feeling of unease from being in Amsterdam, I decided to launch straight in after breakfast. So, from The Shelter, I wound my way back to the Central Station, where the forecourt was crowded with young people sitting, lying, talking and smoking in groups. Rock music blared from radios and guitars, and the smell of marijuana could be detected in the cool January air.

I found my way into the station building, where a parade of shops ran under the central walkway that linked the platforms. Finding a vacant photo booth, I stepped inside, fed in the relevant coins, and then sat looking impassively at the mirror screen opposite as the machine flashed off my passport portrait.

When they'd been taken, I pulled back the curtain, stepped outside – and held up my hands in fake horror. 'My bags, they've gone. Someone's stolen my bags!' I cried in a loud voice. Looking frantically from side to side I began to run round the station, looking everywhere for my non-existent bags. Travellers stopped and looked at me oddly as I ran round crying: 'Help, please. Someone's stolen my things!'

I must have put on a convincing performance, though. I spotted a policeman and ran up to him with a look of mock despair on my face. 'My bags; they've gone. I put them outside the photo booth while I had my pictures taken, and they've gone!' I exclaimed to him.

He shrugged his shoulders with an air of fatality. 'What d'you expect in Amsterdam?' he said resignedly. I was overjoyed; he'd accepted my story at face value. The officer directed me to the nearest police station, where I poured out my story again, careful to try to present a picture of someone distracted and distressed by the loss of all their worldly possessions.

With the 'crime' duly reported and logged, I headed back to the Central Station. Then I made my call to the Nottingham insurance office, carefully injecting a note of panic into my voice as I told how my trip to Spain had been ruined by this terrible theft. I'd been expecting to be told that a cheque would be sent over straight away – but instead they said there was an overseas office of the company in Amsterdam itself; I should go and report there.

For a moment my resolve wavered; had they rumbled me? But then the compulsion to begin our spiritual search overwhelmed me again, and I set off for the address given to me over the phone. It was an expensive-looking suite in a fashionable old Dutch town house alongside one of the attractive tourist stretches of canal. The moment I stepped in the front door, I sensed that my shiny-worn blue suit, polo-neck sweater, long hair and moustache didn't set quite the right tone.

My fears seemed to be confirmed when, after brazenly running through my script for the third time, the enquiries clerk told me: 'Just wait a few minutes would you, please?' He left me sitting at the reception desk as he disappeared into a back office, and I feared that perhaps he had seen through my lies. Maybe he was fetching the police even as I sat there, wondering what to do?

A few minutes later he returned with another man. I was relieved when I saw that he wasn't in uniform – and then alarmed when he introduced himself as a claims investigator. Still, I was there, I reasoned, so I simply had to stick it out. I went through my story again, slowly and carefully, my brain whirring to try to make sure that I didn't alter the facts and trip myself up in the retelling. For an hour and a quarter they asked me questions and more questions, while I tried to remain as calm and innocent as I could.

Finally they telephoned my mother to verify my story. I could have kissed her! She didn't know enough to do other than confirm what I had told them. Her son was travelling on the Continent and had some friends in Spain that he might be going to see, she told them. The claims investigator put the phone down, and turned to me with a smile.

'Well, Mr Goodfellow, I'm sorry that we've kept you so long. Everything seems in order.' He arranged for the cheque for my claim to be made out, and as he handed it over he said by way of apology: 'You can't be too careful these days, you know.'

I waved a hand away in acceptance of his remarks. 'It's OK. I quite understand – you've got to be sure about these things.'

Outside the door I resisted the impulse to hold the cheque to my lips and kiss it. Instead I tucked it into my inside pocket and headed back to The Shelter to report on the successful completion of the first stage in our four-part swindle.

Next day, encouraged by my fraud, Alan, Gary and Mac spent the day taking trains to their foreign cities, pantomiming thefts, reporting them and then returning to Amsterdam. I waited with growing impatience and discomfort; there was something about Amsterdam that was getting under my skin. Almost an apprehension, a sense of foreboding that something dreadfully important, or importantly dreadful, was going to happen soon.

My frustration increased as it became clear that we weren't going to be able to complete the other three frauds so swiftly. Their insurance companies didn't have overseas offices, and the Nottingham branches weren't happy about sending on cheques for such large amounts without completing some detailed paperwork. It was going to be at least a week before payments would be posted on to Amsterdam.

We resigned ourselves to the wait and spent long hours walking the streets, drinking beer in dark, small 'brown bars' along the canal-way streets, and scoring dope from some of the young travellers we met. Passing the time in this way was turning out to be expensive, and I grew more and more concerned and uptight as I saw the money I had made being frittered away so wastefully.

Then, trooping down the stairs at The Shelter one night, ready to head out to wander round and kill the hours before sleep, my eyes caught a small notice pinned to the wall behind the reception area: 'Free Music at The Ark!'

We decided to go and investigate.

The Ij, the river that divides north and south sectors of Amsterdam and ultimately winds its way out to the

North Sea, slaps up against the harbour front at the rear of the Central Station. The water even sounds cold as it slops against the wall beside us as we follow the directions we've been given on this icy, black winter's night.

The Ark turns out to be the two hulking old house-boats lashed together and moored at the end of a line of floating homes, furthest from the station. They sit squat and low on the water line, and look rather uninviting. But as we draw nearer we can hear sounds – warm and welcoming – drifting towards us.

At the door there's a man with shoulder-length white hair, parted down the centre, and a huge grin breaking out from within an equally snowy beard. We reach for our pockets and make gestures about paying for entrance, but he just smiles at us even more broadly and waves us in. 'It's OK; it's free. Welcome to The Ark!'

Ducking our heads, we drop down through the door into the main room of the longboat. It's a room that runs back thirty feet or more into the distance, and that's where most of the noise is coming from: a rock band pounding out some contemporary rhythms. Sitting around the floor are perhaps forty or so young traveller types, bunched around low-level tables scattered across the room. Like one of those 'spot the difference' quizzes I run the scene through my brain and instantly realise what's missing from a near-normal scene: there isn't a single beer bottle to be found. And at the same time I notice that there are only a few spirals of smoke – and none make my nose wrinkle in the way you expect dope to. I'm confused: this is a picture I'm used to, but it's not quite right somehow.

As I lead the four of us into the room, I'm approached by a slip of a girl. She's no more than five feet four, with long, blonde hair, a fresh, open face, and a smile to match the guy at the door. But it's her eyes that unnerve me. Big and blue, they seem to bore straight into me, right into my heart, as she looks up at me welcomingly. It's an uncomfortable feeling, almost as though she can see right into everything I've ever done, and I find myself unwillingly dropping my gaze to the floor as she says: 'Hi.'

She's small and vulnerable compared to my size and frame, yet I'm the one who feels intimidated, unnerved by the encounter. There's an awkward silence for a moment or two, and all the old feelings of insecurity and fear start to slip back into focus.

She introduces herself as Sherry, and says that she lives here on the boats as part of a Christian community with other people from ten or more different nations. I can hear the words, but somehow they're not really registering; they're flying somewhere over the top of my head.

'Yeah, that's great ... er, where's the beer?'

'Oh, we don't do that kind of thing,' she returns casually. 'We don't need to get drunk any more.'

A glimmer of hope. 'Oh, what about pills, then? What do you take?'

She smiles gently and says: 'No, you don't understand. We're Christians, you see ...' and she begins to explain to me how she and her friends belong to Jesus now.

Suddenly I'm seized by a terrifying, overwhelming sense of suffocation. I don't know what she's going on about, but I know that if I don't get out of this place now, this moment, I'm going to die. I can almost feel thick, strong fingers closing round my throat. I've got to get away from this weird, off-centre place, and this strange, peaceful-yet-powerful young woman.

I turn round, back to the others, who have been hovering a few paces back, looking round the room, as I have this short exchange with Sherry. Thankfully they don't seem to have picked up my alarm, my feelings of fear and vulnerability.

'No dope, lads, no beer either. There's nothing here for us; let's go find somewhere else,' I tell them, and we turn and tumble out up onto the pierside again.

The Paradiso was like a refuge after The Ark. Crammed with people stoned out of their heads, thick with smoke and awash with beer and pills, it pulsed to loud acid rock. We found a table and worked our way steadily into near oblivion, me trying to wash away the uncomfortable feelings I'd had from our brief visit to the houseboats.

Hours later, as we slumped on the floor, letting the music roll over us like breakers on the seashore, I remembered that night in Canada, when I'd seen my life flash before me, and thought again how close to the edge I must be.

The infamous Paradiso—renowned throughout Europe —soothed me for a few hours, but when I woke late the next morning in The Shelter – we'd got back really late, and aroused the ire of the caretaker by calling him from his bed – the sense of impending doom was on me even more strongly than ever.

I couldn't wait around any longer. I told the others that we had to make a move that very day. We'd push the claims along as much as we could on the phone, and then we'd leave Amsterdam for good. Mac knew someone who lived in a small town not far away; we could go and stay there until the money finally came through. Anything was better than staying in that creepy city a moment longer!

I'd just stepped out of one of the phone booths at the station, after arranging the alternative accommodation. We were bending to pick up our bags and head for the bus, when a voice called out: 'Hi, remember me? It's Sherry. We met last night at The Ark. D'you remember?'

I turned and there she was, smiling as broadly as before, and not seeming to be at all uncomfortable or put out by the fact that I'd brought our previous conversation to an abrupt end by turning and walking away from her in mid-sentence. 'Looks like you're leaving the city, eh? What've you guys been doing, then?'

I made some non-committal response, but Sherry
didn't seem deterred by my determined indifference.
She told us brightly that she'd only bumped into us
because she'd left her purse behind, and had been
heading back to The Ark to pick it up when she saw us.
'You must at least let me buy you all a hamburger and a
coffee before you leave Amsterdam.'

Almost before we knew what had happened, we had
shouldered our bags and were following her down to
the city's flea market, where the five of us squeezed
round a small table in a crowded cafeteria. We didn't
speak, but we all seemed to have been similarly knocked
back by Sherry's cheerful warmth and openness – and,
besides, with money short we weren't about to turn
down the offer of a free meal. As I bit into my burger,
I couldn't help thinking how self-possessed and confident she was to trust herself to the company of four
rough-and-ready customers like us – and I envied her
composure.

After telling us a little more of what she was doing in
the city, she asked again: 'So what's brought you here?'

We all chewed silently for a few minutes. Finally I
decided that I'd tell her straight. I swallowed. 'Well,
Sherry, we're travelling through to the East. We've set
out on a journey to find God.'

The laughter I'd half anticipated never came. Instead
she seemed genuinely excited by what I'd said. I told her
more about our experiences and conversations, with the
other three chipping in as I progressed. We brought her
right up to date: '... and so we're on a kind of pilgrimage, if you like, to discover God.'

Sherry was the first person we'd ever spoken to who
didn't dismiss us as cranks. Indeed she seemed to
identify with what we were saying. Over the course of
the next two hours, and further coffees, she told us of
her own search for God, for truth, for meaning, and
how it had been resolved when she found 'the Lord'.

All the growing excitement I'd been feeling that here

was a kindred spirit evaporated when she began to tell
us that she was a Christian, a disciple of Jesus; that he
was God and that she loved him. How sad, I thought.
She'd fallen for all the fairy stories and the falsehoods
that I'd left locked up in St Patrick's.

Several coffees later she told us that she really had to
make a move, but if we weren't doing anything in the
evening, we could join her for supper at The Ark. It
would be fun, she said, to talk some more.

Our eyes followed Sherry as she walked off with a
friendly wave, and I think in some ways we'd all fallen in
love with her. We began to chatter all at once about this
incredible girl: someone who was really interested in us,
who recognised the longings we had inside, who didn't
laugh at us, who wasn't afraid of us, who accepted us as
we were – even if she was sadly misguided about God.
What made her like that?

None of us had the answer to that, but we knew two
things. We weren't leaving Amsterdam after all. And we
had a date at The Ark.

10

Coming Home

The afternoon couldn't pass quickly enough for us. We spent the time trying to decide among ourselves why this sweet, innocent-looking girl should take the time and trouble to befriend us. What was it all about? We decided not to touch any drink or drugs, because we didn't want to disappoint Sherry by turning up with our brains in orbit and exhibiting sky-high smiles.

At the same time, despite the excitement we'd all felt inside as she'd identified with our own inner hunger, I was feeling cautious. Even with the prospect of some sort of answer within my grasp, I didn't feel able to reach out and take hold of it. I feared that such a move would expose me, make me vulnerable and weak in the others' eyes. So when we arrived at The Ark at the appropriate time, I tried to affect an air of casual disregard – about as successfully as a fox might if presented with a trussed chicken. If the guy at the door – the same bearded watchman as the previous night – detected my mask of uninterest, he didn't show it. He just grinned broadly again and welcomed us in.

Sherry was there, smiling and pleased to see us. She guided us through and across to the second houseboat, moored alongside. We stepped over and down into a large kitchen area, where a team of long-haired cooks were bustling round a range stacked with frying pans and pots. It smelled good. From there Sherry led us into the main dining room, where there was a large central table with spaces for about forty people.

'This is the main eating area,' she told us, guiding us to seats. 'We live on this boat – there are dormitories right below, and this is where we invite people to come and spend time with us.' We sat down awkwardly, a little nervous about all the other unfamiliar faces around us. Sherry introduced us to a young man sitting nearby, as people took their places. 'This is Peter Gruschka. He lives on The Ark, too.'

The hubbub of laughter and chatter died away, and I looked up to one end of the table to follow everyone else's gaze. I couldn't quite believe my eyes. Standing up, looking round the room with a broad grin, was just about the tallest guy I had ever seen. He towered about six feet six inches, and the low ceiling of the boat just seemed to accentuate his height. I half thought he might crack his head if he stood up too quickly. Equally striking was his dress – white from head to foot in a baggy, Indian-style shirt and long, baggy trousers. With his long sandy hair, centre-parted and down to his shoulders, his beard, moustache and leather sandals, he reminded me of a larger-than-life version of the Jesus picture that had hung in our home.

'That's Floyd McClung. He leads the community here,' Sherry whispered to me in explanation as the tall guy began to speak. He welcomed everyone to The Ark, and then asked people to introduce their guests. I realised that we four weren't the only strangers, and I cringed with embarrassment as Sherry stood up to tell our names and how she'd come to meet us. I wanted to slip quietly under the table so that no one could see me, but as I looked round they just smiled 'nice to see you' looks at us.

'OK, let's give thanks,' Floyd said, and bowed his head. I looked round and noticed that everyone else had followed suit, so I ducked my head. Then I realised that he was praying over the food. It was the first time I'd ever sat down at a table without diving straight into the meal, and I wondered why we had to wait. Floyd prayed

briefly and without fuss, and then sat down as the food
was brought out to be served. Soon the air was filled
with conversation and chuckles again, and I thought
momentarily how people had never seemed as relaxed
after prayers when I'd gone to church all those years.

The food was good, and it was free, so we piled in.
Concentrating on eating enabled me to avoid more than
the briefest word of response to the questions and
comments from some of those sitting nearby. As I
chewed I felt my old paranoia and insecurity rising
quickly. I desperately wished that I'd dropped some
speed or sipped a few beers before coming; at least that
would have given me some confidence to get through
the visit. As it was I felt frightened – like a little boy at a
new school – and yet at the same time I sensed how
confident and at ease Sherry was alongside me. The
contrast hit me hard: the world-weary man who'd seen it
all, unable to mumble more than a word or two; and the
naive and youthful girl seemingly self-possessed and
calm. What did she have that I didn't?

By the time the meal was over I was feeling more and
more uncomfortable – and also desperate for a cigarette.
It had been a long time since I'd gone more than an
hour without lighting up, and I was itching to reach for
my packet. But it stayed in my pocket, because as I
looked round I couldn't find anybody else smoking, and
there was a conspicuous absence of ashtrays. Never
mind, I thought, we'll soon be able to get outside.

But then the people sitting round the table started
to pass books along. Sherry handed one to me and
I turned the brown-covered volume over. 'The New
Testament' it said on the front. The tall guy stood up
again and began to read from one of the gospels inside.
Sherry turned to the page for me. I listened and
followed the words on the page curiously; it didn't mean
a thing to me. Then he spoke briefly about the passage
we'd just looked at, and I wondered how on earth he'd
found the things he was talking about in what we'd just

read. Maybe I'd been looking at the wrong page or
something?

Before I knew it, most of the young men and women
sitting around had started singing. They all seemed to
know the words off by heart – something to do with
God's love – and they smiled as they looked around and
sang. I didn't know whether to laugh or hide my face in
embarrassment, so I looked down at the table and
breathed a long, slow sigh of relief when they finished
and the supper party broke up.

Everyone seemed to have a job to do, and no one
seemed to mind. Plates and cups were gathered, tables
and chairs cleared and wiped down, dishes washed and
dried. The clearing up was carried out with a cheerful
air of organisation. Meanwhile Sherry and Peter led me
and the others over to a group of big old armchairs,
where we flopped down and looked at each other. For a
few minutes Sherry and Peter talked to us some more
about 'the Lord', whose name we'd heard repeatedly in
the conversations going on around us at suppertime. We
nodded and made non-committal responses, and were
relieved when a little later came the opportunity for us
to say thanks, but it was really time we were heading
back to our hostel for the night.

Out on the harbour front, drawing heavily on much-
needed tobacco, we buried each other under questions.
What had we made of all of that? Did you see the freaky
tall guy in the white robes? What was all this talk about
Christianity – the only Christians we'd ever met were a
bunch of hypocrites. Was there maybe something in all
their talk of God and his love for the world? How could
anyone really have their act together and yet still believe
in Jesus? Could this be what we were looking for? Our
discussions continued late into the night. Contrary to
our expectations, dope and drink didn't help shed any
further light on things.

For all the awkwardness I'd felt while I was actually
there, I'd come away sensing that there was something

in the atmosphere of The Ark that I couldn't do without. So we quickly accepted their offer to go back again. We returned the following evening – and nightly, over the next week. Each time there were smiling and friendly faces, great rushes of vulnerability and the promise of something fantastic. It was a curious mix of something I couldn't stand to be near, but couldn't bear being away from either.

Eventually I decided that the answer must lie in the fact that they were on something. Maybe the big fellow, the ringleader, had a secret supply of some kind of superdrug stashed away below decks. Peter had always been particularly friendly when we arrived, so I dared to ask him one evening.

'Come on, what are you all taking? What are you on?'

He looked at me and smiled widely. Clapping me on the shoulder with a hearty laugh he replied: 'We're on Jesus, I guess. That's all!'

I wasn't really sure what he meant. But I believed him. I had a gut feeling that he'd been telling me the truth – whatever it was.

During our visits, Sherry and her friends continued to talk with us in broad terms about God and the world, and what we thought life was all about. We looked forward to these conversations because we hoped they might provide some understanding in our search, but even more compelling was the intangible sense of welcome we felt. These people were for real. It was good to feel cared for.

This feeling of identity made us leap at their offer of going to live on board The Ark as part of the community, even more than the prospect of further talks about God. Just being part of a group of people who really cared for each other was attractive. We decided that we'd like to spend some time on The Ark before finally setting out for our gurus in the East.

Before that, though, we had some business to attend to back in Nottingham. The other three had been told that their insurance claims would only be paid out if they applied personally for them back in England, and the final third of my claim was awaiting payment on similar grounds. We decided to risk going home for a few days to complete our swindle.

But we couldn't shake the impression that The Ark folk had made on us. Back in the Midlands we told Sarah and Jenny about these amazing people we'd met, and how they'd asked us to go and live with them. They said they'd like to come, too, but we said we'd better ask to see if it was OK before they set out. We agreed to call them as soon as we could after we'd returned to Amsterdam.

When I went to claim my outstanding monies, I found myself facing another long interview with a claims investigator. They gave me the cheque for what was still due under my claim, and then asked me to return the following day to complete a few formalities. I sensed that they were on to me, and I reasoned that when I turned up the next morning there would be a policeman or two waiting to arrest me and take me away. In a panic I packed my bags, called the other three, and told them I was flying out to Amsterdam first thing in the morning.

As the plane dropped in to land at Schipol Airport I was seized by a sense of foreboding that forced me back into my seat with rigid fear: I was going to die in this Dutch city! Breaking out in a cold sweat, I tried to pray for the first time since a child, searching in my memory for the words of the 'Our Father'. But I realised that I didn't know what to say, or who to say it to, and as I grappled with a feeling that I was abandoned and lost, the wheels touched down with a gentle bump and we were there.

Back in Amsterdam, my excitement turned to apprehension. What if they'd changed their minds, and they wouldn't let me in? I spent a couple of hours walking round the canals and narrow side streets before I finally plucked up the courage to go and knock on The Ark's big, broad door. It opened to another big smile. 'Hey, it's John Goodfellow, isn't it? Welcome back – and come on in.'

Alan, Gary and Mac arrived a couple of days later with their payments and similar stories of the suspicion that they had been rumbled. But we figured that the police would never be able to trace us to these big old hulks out the back of Amsterdam's Central Station and, besides, pretty soon we'd be off overland in a beat-up van. They would never catch us!

We were welcomed onto The Ark as part of the guest list; there were about a dozen of us outsiders altogether who'd been invited to spend some time living on board. Those who lived there full time explained the routine we were expected to fit into: breakfast communally at 7.30 am, followed by a couple of hours of jobs around the boats – washing, repairing, maintaining, cooking. Then, at mid-morning, we all met together in the main room for what they called their Family Time. Over an hour or so they'd sing a few songs, pray and then Floyd McClung would talk from the Bible about what it meant to live as a Christian.

Gradually I found these times less intimidating and awkward, and while I still didn't really understand what they were all going on about, I was happy to clap along and even try to join in with the occasional song that I picked up from its repetition. The religious talk all seemed a bit remote, but I could put up with it because it was all part of something much wider and deeper – a thrilling, heart-warming, tingling sense of belonging and purpose that seemed to emanate from everyone there. It seemed to me that most of the people around me felt it, and although I didn't, I knew that it existed, and I knew that I wanted it for myself, too! From time to time I would slip away of an evening with the other three to brood over a couple of beers. None of us could put our finger on it, but we all agreed that there was a pulse of real, hard hope beating in us for the first time we could remember.

I'm sitting cross-legged on the floor in a Family Time and relaxing into the familiar flow of a simple song. It's short and expressive, and as I look around I pause to think how the faces seem to shine with its meaning. To me it's just a nice song, but to them there seems somehow to be something more, as though they're not just singing the words — they're telling them *to* someone, or something. The room fills with joyful, enthusiastic voices and the accompaniment of clapping hands and bongo drums.

I snap my head in a shake of disbelief as suddenly a symphony of additional sound breaks into my hearing. It's like thousands of other voices — majestic and proud — have suddenly joined in with our small group. It's so clear and close that I guess someone must have switched on a tape machine or the radio or something, so I twist from side to side. No audio equipment in sight. Everyone else is concentrating on singing; they don't seem to have noticed anything out of the ordinary.

Before I can even start to make sense of this strange sensation, I'm pitched face forwards. The voices of the hidden singers splash into and mix with those of the people around me as I feel myself being doubled over by some kind of wave. And I burst into tears, beginning to sob in gut-wrenching spasms that tear their way out of somewhere deep in the very centre of my being.

It's all happening so suddenly and unexpectedly that I'm almost able to stand back and watch it all — yet at the same time I'm caught up in the very centre. My brain's racing and I'm asking, 'What's happening?' as the tears start to stream down my face, with great gasps of anguish. A detached thought that everyone around me will think that I've cracked up is washed away as the river of emotion continues to burst the banks of my heart. And as the singing gently continues, almost unconcernedly, I feel as though the release of all those pent-up tears have left the real me, deep inside, grounded on firm land. I'm seeing myself as I really am, and it's awful.

Selfish, arrogant, spiteful, vicious, uncaring, proud. The realisation hammers into me. All these years of self-justification, deceit, excuses and avoidance, simply fall away. I see that I've hurt, robbed, cheated, lied, abused and damaged without defence. 'They wouldn't miss the money; she'd been asking for it; he'd hurt me; I needed it.' All these excuses don't matter. It's my life. They're my decisions. There is no one to blame but myself; nowhere to turn with the finger of accusation other than inwards.

From fingertip to toe, head to heel, I'm rotten, filthy and wicked. I'm still weeping uncontrollably, but the initial embarrassment is being replaced by a feeling of relief and welcome. It's all over; I don't have to pretend any more. My tears feel like they're washing away the dirt from my insides.

I look up and over at Floyd sitting on the other side of the room. They're still singing around me, and he reaches into his pocket and passes something to the person alongside. Hand to hand it comes round to me: a big, white handkerchief. As I press my face gratefully into its pure, clean freshness I look over and see him smiling at me with a nod of understanding. It's like he knows what this weird experience is all about, and yet he's saying that he accepts me without question.

Someone puts an arm around me as the sobs subside and whispers: 'It's OK, John, we understand, we understand.'

Which is more than I do. I know this is all about the very essence of my life, but I can't explain it.

The understanding came later. In the days that followed, some of the things that Floyd talked about began to take some sort of shape in my head. And Peter and some of the other Ark community talked to me more directly about their God and his world.

They told me how God had created man in his image, and had intended the world to be a beautiful place of harmony and peace where he and his creation could enjoy each other for ever. But man had rebelled against God's order – he wilfully disobeyed – and that had brought an awful separation between the Creator and his created being.

The Bible explained that everyone had gone wrong, that no one was perfect. So God had sent Jesus into the world to 'pay the price' of our wrongdoing, so that we could be re-united with God. The penalty for all our sin was death, and Jesus, who had lived a sinless life on earth, had been crucified to take the punishment we deserved. But he'd risen from death, defeating the power of sin once and for all, and now everyone who believed in him could be set free from their old life, and begin a new spiritual life that would go on for eternity.

They explained to me that only God's Holy Spirit could bring people to an understanding of these things, and that he had been at work in my life, fracturing the dam of my walled-up emotions during that Family Time. And they said that they'd been praying for this to happen since I'd arrived at The Ark, content to await God's timing to tell me more about him.

This picture was painted for me carefully and gently during the course of long conversations over the next few days. The more I asked, the more they explained, and I felt like a whole new world was opening up in front of me. I was eager to talk about what they believed and what it might mean for my life. But there was one blockage. I accepted all they told me about Jesus – how he was fully God, yet at the same time fully man, and that he'd risen from the grave and now lived for ever – but I just couldn't believe that God had created the world in the first place. It was just too much for me. Until one morning.

Alan, Mac and I were putting our bricklaying expertise to good use by building a small wall round the waste-pipes leading down the back of the boats. We'd dug the hole, laid out the site, and were setting the bricks down in place when it struck me how easily we had made plans and constructed something. With simple logic I then told myself if we – created beings – could design and make something, then a supreme being – God – could surely design and make a world. It felt as though I'd won the pools!

Standing on the top of the half-built wall, I shouted down to Gary who was also below: 'That's it! I understand now. God did make the world! I believe, Gary, I believe!' He looked up at me quizzically as though I'd finally flipped as I grinned hugely. 'That's it! I believe, I believe!' I dropped my trowel and shovel and ran inside, shouting to the others my discovery. 'I know it's true. I believe!'

Later that day I knelt down beside my bunk in the small dormitory room below deck. Despite the heaters it was always cold and slightly damp down there below the waterline, but I didn't notice this time. As the water lapped against the wall a few inches from my head I began to pray for only the second time in my adult life – but this time I knew someone was there.

'O Jesus, I know you're real. I'm so sorry for all the dreadful things I've done in my life . . .' and I slowly and methodically began to list my misdeeds. During one of my conversations with Peter he'd said that becoming a Christian meant you had to confess all your sins – and I didn't want to miss a single one out. By the time I'd admitted everything I could remember, a long time had passed. Then I asked him to come into my life. 'Jesus, I believe that you are the Son of God, and that you died to take away my sins. And I believe that you can forgive me and give me a new life as your child. Please come into my life right now. I've made such a mess of it that I want you to take charge. Please help me. I've hurt so many people in so many ways. Please change my heart, and take away all the anger and the bitterness. Make me a new person, like you promise. I want what you've given all the others.'

I stopped talking, and slumped forward with my head on my bed. Then a ripple of calm, secure peace ran down my body. I was sure that my prayer had been answered.

Somehow I managed to go up to supper disguising the excited smile that wanted to break out on my face. I kept my secret until after the meal. Then I stood up and announced the words I had heard several times before from other visitors to The Ark, but which had always left me mystified: 'I've been born again!'

I was swamped by cheers, shouts of congratulations and slaps on the back. Then everyone started to sing a song of praise to God, and for the first time I was able to join in and feel that I was a part of it.

I had been away for a long, long time, but now it felt like I was coming home.

11

First Steps

It wasn't long before I knew that something truly dramatic had happened. With the warmth of my 'welcome' still surrounding me, I slipped downstairs to my bunk and reached for my jacket pocket. As I pulled out the packet of cigarettes that I always turned to for an after-meal smoke, I realised that things were different this time. My hands had acted out of habit, but I discovered that I didn't want to smoke.

It wasn't that I didn't think I ought to – everything was still so new to me that I hadn't even begun to attempt to think through the implications my new-found faith would have on my lifestyle. All I knew was that for the first time in a dozen years I had absolutely no desire to pull blasts of nicotine into my chest. I turned the packet over in my hand as I looked at it curiously. Then I wandered up on deck, flipped the packet over in my palm a few times, and then flicked it out into the grey water.

I watched it float on the surface for a couple of minutes before it filled with water and sank away. The desire had gone. It was just as though someone had removed it under anaesthetic. I hadn't felt any pain. This previously important part of my life had simply been cut away! Over the next couple of nights it became clear that the same had happened with drink and drugs. This about-turn was perhaps even more remarkable, considering I had been an alcoholic and addict for so many years. But when one of the others would come over to my bunk at night and whisper that we could slip into town and score some dope or have a few beers, I simply didn't want to go.

Yet whatever operation it was that had been performed wasn't so much an amputation as a transplant. I found that in place of my thirst for smoking, getting stoned and drinking was the need to drink in the Bible. All the passages I'd heard read and discussed over the previous weeks came flooding back into my thoughts, and I desperately wanted to read them for myself. I found myself poring over the Bible for a couple of hours at a stretch, completely absorbed by what I was reading, and it was making sense for the first time. I felt as though suddenly I had a personal stake in all that was written there. While the words had once been distant and detached, they were now crucially important. My heart would start racing in excited anticipation every time I'd turn again to one of the well-thumbed Bibles lying around The Ark.

I'd spent so much of my life in a fog of confused thoughts and emotions. Now I knew from the clarity with which I viewed everything and everyone around me that a change of momentous proportions had taken place. And with the help of some of the male workers on The Ark, I began to explore what it meant. We spent long hours talking about how becoming a Christian wasn't just about turning your back on an old life, but starting a whole new one; and that God had a personal plan for me that he wanted to unfold.

About three nights after my tea-time admission of conversion, I was sitting up late talking with two new friends when they began to explain to me how Jesus was coming back again soon. It sounded really exciting. They told me that the Bible taught that Jesus would one day return to this world, and he would be recognised by everyone as the sovereign Lord of the universe. No one would be able to deny his majesty and authority. I began to thrill to their description, and was waiting to hear more when it happened again – another 'wave' crashed into me from behind, doubling me forward from the waist.

At the same time I felt a beautiful, sweet warmth ripple over and down and through my body, just as though someone had poured perfumed oil all over me. It was a glorious moment, as I was bathed in this honey of love. The sheer richness of the tenderness I felt all over me reduced me to tears again and I started sobbing – but this time gently and gratefully. Before I'd been a little unsure about my response; this time I simply enjoyed the liberation and freedom of being able to weep unashamedly and thankfully. I felt my own heart melting inside me, responding to the warmth in which I was engulfed; layers of indifference and selfishness were falling away before the presence of God's care and concern.

My head was bowed, but without looking up I sensed that someone was standing above me. Jesus. With hands, wounded and welcoming, open before me. No words were needed, but he spoke clearly, straight into my heart: 'John, you belong to me now. You are mine. I accept you and I love you. John, you are mine.'

In a moment my awareness of this powerful presence was gone, and I continued to weep quietly in wonder and thankfulness. I'd known I needed God's forgiveness for all the evil there had been in my life. Now I knew for a certainty that he had granted it for one simple reason. Because he loved me. I didn't deserve it. I could never repay it. But he loved me, totally and selflessly. It was a wonderful moment, and as I looked up to the two men who had sat by quietly as I bowed to God's love, one of them reached over to hug me. I gripped him firmly in response, with genuine affection, glad to be able to share this moment. Even as I did so I realised what a change had come over me here. For the first time I could recall I felt comfortable sharing emotions with someone else. I thought how great it was to be part of a real family for the first time. God's family.

Somehow I floated down to my bunk later that night, drifting off to sleep finally in a warm haze. I woke early the next morning still intoxicated by the awareness of God's accepting love. Wrapping a thick coat around me I slipped out onto the deck and paced up and down for a couple of hours until other sounds of life stirred below. 'I love you, Jesus. I love you,' I whispered over and over again as I walked up and down. It felt good to say it.

The following days saw no let-up in excitement. Sometimes the inexplicable joy that seemed to well up inside me threatened to make me burst. I revelled in the brightness and freshness I found in everything. Even the ordinary, everyday things like rainstorms and meal-times became a source of fascination and delight as I'd think how God was behind them. They hadn't just come about by accident; they were all a part of God's marvellous plan in shaping this world! It was as though the projector of my life had previously only been able to screen dull black-and-white. Now everything was in glorious Technicolor, and the mundane suddenly became magical.

A couple of weeks later, Gary and I were baptised in a small chapel in an Amsterdam backstreet. Gary had made his own, private peace with God a few days after me. The congregation knew the work of The Ark well and often loaned their pool for the baptism of new converts. We joined with about half a dozen others in giving a short account of our new walk with Jesus, before being lowered under the water and raised up to jubilant singing and clapping.

The newness of everything was so overwhelming for a while that I almost forgot that there was life beyond The Ark. When I finally remembered that we'd arrived on the run from the police, I knew that this was one of the many things I had to sort out now that I had a new life as part of God's family. I went to Floyd one morning and told him rather sheepishly that we'd come to the boats a little under false pretences, and I filled him in with the story. In the short time we'd been there, we'd seen all types coming along – drug addicts, alcoholics, psychotics – but I knew we'd been wrong to mislead them. Floyd didn't seem disturbed by what I told him – he was more interested in what was going to happen next.

He explained that it was up to me. I had decisions to make. But as we talked, he showed me how in the Bible it said that when a thief became a Christian, he should pay back the money he had taken, and live a peaceable life. Later, in my bunk, I flipped through my Bible to find the verse myself, tucked away in Ephesians chapter 4. 'It's pretty clear what you've got to do, John,' I thought to myself as I re-read the sentence. The next morning I sought Floyd out.

'I've decided. I believe that I should go back and confess to all the things I've done wrong, and try to put them right.'

Floyd nodded and smiled. 'I think you're right, John,' he agreed quietly. Later that afternoon, we both borrowed bicycles and pedalled over to the insurance office where I'd made my original false claim. Floyd didn't seem to notice the strange looks given to the cycling, long-haired giant as he strode in and explained briefly on my behalf why we were there.

The man behind the counter eyed me up and down closely, and said that he remembered me. He told me that he knew my claim had been fraudulent, because detectives had been in recently to interview him about it.

'Well, about three weeks ago I became a Christian,' I told him. 'I know what I did was wrong, and I'm planning to go back to England to confess, and I want to pay all the money back.'

He dropped the formal air with which he had been acting, clearly surprised by my openness. After taking a few details down on a scrap of paper he bade us farewell. 'I've never heard anything like this before in my life,' he said, shaking his head with a smile. 'Good luck!'

I knew that it wasn't a decision I could leave to 'luck'.

Before, I'd dreaded having to wake up and get out of bed each morning. But now coursing through my veins was a heady sense of God's love and care for me, which brought me bursting into each new day.

I'd fallen in love, and I wanted to show how much I cared in whatever way I could; putting right some of my mistakes of the past seemed to be the right place to start.

My crimes hadn't only been committed out in the streets, though. I knew that a good many had taken place at home, within the four walls of the Goodfellow household: the bitterness, jealousy, resentment and anger. I wondered quite how I could tackle this history of hurt, but I knew that I wanted my family to know the exciting new life I'd discovered. One night I called home, and over a crackling line told Mum hastily that I'd met some great people. I said that I'd become a Christian, and I was coming home soon to sort a few things out.

She was confused. 'What d'you mean, Johnny? I don't understand. The police have been round here looking for you. What have you been up to? You're not in any trouble are you, son?'

I tried to explain what had happened. 'It's OK, Mum. I've become a Christian. These people here are going to help me. Everything's going to be OK. Honest.'

'What do you mean, you've become a Christian, Johnny? You've always been a Christian, son. Your father and I took you to church for years. What are you talking about?' She sounded anxious and a little baffled.

I didn't know where to begin. It was hopeless trying to express on the phone this revolution in my world. 'I know I went to church for years, Mum, but I never knew Jesus. But I've met him now. He's alive!'

Our conversation ended unsatisfactorily, and I ached to be able to see her face to face and explain. But instead of allowing my frustrations to get the better of me, I punched some more coins into the money slot and dialled the other number on my list. It was the central police station in Nottingham.

It quickly became clear that it wasn't every day someone rang up from overseas admitting they've committed a crime, and trying to arrange to come home to face the music! But eventually I managed to speak to someone in the Criminal Investigation Department who knew of my case, and we arranged details of when I'd be travelling home on the ferry. Officers would be waiting to arrest me as I stepped ashore.

The next few days sped by in a blur of happiness and anticipation. I couldn't express what I felt inside, but it was like all the Christmas Eves of my youth rolled into one: those wonderful hours of expectancy – before arguments shattered the peace – when I lay in bed knowing, hoping that something wonderful was going to begin soon, and wishing it closer. I spent all my waking hours reading the Bible, talking to Ark workers and asking them the million-and-one questions I had about this new life I'd begun. I sat alongside them, too, in the coffee bar in the evenings as they talked about Jesus with visitors. I desperately wanted to join in, but I was too embarrassed at what these streetwise sceptics might make of my naive faith.

I'm standing outside the Central Station, and it's hard to believe how much has happened in just a few short weeks. I can see over to the spot, a few yards away, where the turn-around began; where we were planning to leave the city and start our pilgrimage to the East, when Sherry bumped into us because of a missing purse. It makes me warm inside to think that even then, when I didn't realise it, God was more concerned about finding us than we were about finding him.

But as I pause to consider the different departure I'm planning now, the euphoria evaporates. In a little while I'm due to catch a train to the ferry to go back and give myself up to the police. I know God is with me – I'm sure of it with every fibre in my being – but I'm rather anxious all the same. I sit down on a bench and turn to the Bible that in such a short space of time has already begun to feel so at home, so satisfying, in my hand. I still don't know my way around this fascinating, exciting, confusing, shocking book of books, so it's by no design of mine that I find myself somewhere in Isaiah, and reading a passage that seems to spring off the page at me.

'When you pass through the waters, I will be with you … you will not drown. … Fear not, for I will be with you … I have called you by name.'

A jolt of assurance runs through me as I accept this as a message of support for my ferry trip. 'Thank you, Father God, for giving me this encouragement.'

When the approaching English coastline causes me to waver a few hours later, even just for a moment, I know what to do. I turn to my Bible expectantly, hopefully, and once more find my eyes plucking a passage from an unfamiliar page. It's Isaiah again: 'Don't dwell on the former things … I'm making a way in the desert.'

I don't know what is going to happen. I don't know how God is going to work. But I do know that everything is going to be all right. I'm so confident that I'm almost delighted to see the waiting policemen as I come through the terminal building at Harwich. Anyone watching might mistake us for being long-lost relatives!

Having Peter Gruschka sitting alongside me in the police car on the way to the local police station was a wonderfully tangible reminder that I hadn't set off alone.

In the few weeks I'd been on The Ark, he and I had struck up a close friendship. Since that night when I'd knelt beside my bunk and asked Jesus Christ into my life all sorts of things had been happening inside me – it felt like a whole lot of melting, cracking, pounding and dismantling was all going on at the same time. One of the things I knew was that I was finding myself responding to people in a different way – and I had warmed to Peter greatly.

Tall and rangy, with a shock of curly hair, you would probably have counted this easy-going German as one of the visitors rather than staff if you'd peeked into The Ark's crowded coffee bar in the evening. He was still the typical drop-out in many ways, although he'd rejected the drugs-and-sex scene in favour of what he'd found in Jesus.

Before coming to work on The Ark, he'd been a professional actor and singer, touring Europe in the cast of the musical *Hair!* The production was the ultimate statement of the peace and love culture, shocking audiences with its full-frontal nudity, glorification of drugs, and anarchy. During the performance members of the cast would, as well as shedding their clothes, step down off the stage and walk into the auditorium to hand out marijuana to members of the audience.

This was Peter's life – until one night. Finishing a show in Paris, he and a musician friend were leaving the theatre when they met two little old ladies waiting at the rear door, who asked if they could talk for a few minutes. The spinsters began to tell the two long-haired men about how Jesus Christ had come into the world to rescue them from their sins, and to give them a wonderful new life. They didn't leave before handing New Testaments over to the astonished friends.

The encounter made a deep impact on both men, and they later became Christians, and began to share their new faith with other members of the cast. It wasn't long before tracts and New Testaments were being handed round the concert halls instead of dope. Peter was asked to leave – his message wasn't compatible with the show's New Age mysticism. With a burning love for God, and an intimate understanding of others like him he soon found himself working on The Ark.

I loved hearing him tell his life story, and it thrilled me to think that God wanted to perform a similar topsy-turvy act in my life. So when he volunteered to come back to England with me to support me through the various scenes that I would have to face, I was overjoyed. I was also touched that someone would care enough about me to want to put himself to so much trouble. It was another example to me of the selfless love of God I was seeing lived out by people who followed Jesus.

At Harwich police station they viewed us both a little suspiciously to begin with. Finally, though, I was taken into an interview room where I made a full and detailed confession to one of the detectives. He took it all down in longhand as I spoke, and after reading it over and signing it, I was allowed to go free on bail, to await further contact from the police back home in Nottingham.

As Peter and I sat on the train, rattling up the line to the Midlands, my mind kept racing ahead of me. I felt nervous and excited all at the same time. How would my parents respond to the homecoming of the son who had made the family name of Goodfellow a cruel joke for so long?

12

Putting Right the Past

Bursting with excitement, I knocked at the front door. I couldn't wait to see my family – nor for them to see me. In the last few weeks I'd found myself falling in love with them all for the first time properly in my life, and I couldn't wait to look at them with gentleness, in place of that hardness and coldness. And I wanted them to see the difference in me.

I had absolutely no doubt that they would see the change. I was brimming with confidence—not in me, but in the wonderful person I'd discovered: Jesus, who had changed me. I had never known such peace. I was sure that those who had most reason to remember the old me with regret would see the difference. And I was certain that when I explained the how – or, rather, the who – of my transformation, then they would want to invite Jesus into their lives too.

Mum opened the door and I engulfed her in an uncharacteristic hug. She was surprised but pleased, and I went to put my arms round the rest of the family too. It was so good to see them and I realised that the new feelings I had for them were still there. Pretty soon we were all sitting round the table over a noisy tea, and I started to try to tell them all that had happened. From one or two nervous glances I caught out of the corner of my eye, I sensed that it was maybe a bit too soon, so I bit my tongue and instead enjoyed the food. There would be plenty of time afterwards. Chewing and smiling, I had to blink away the tears as I looked round the table at my family.

Their faces were, of course, so familiar. But it was as though I was looking at them through a new pair of eyes. I saw them in a softer light, no longer as people who I felt only wanted to squash me, but as people who had needs and hurts, and wants and pains of their own. There was Dad, tired, proud, self-reliant and lonely. Mum, weary, worried and cheated of the close family she'd longed for. Joan, her young hopes for the glamorous life crumpled, a single parent with old-looking eyes. Trish, in many ways a typical fiery teenager, but also with an angry streak I recognised from my own past.

'Oh, Jesus, I love them so very much,' I whispered silently. 'Thank you for letting me see them more as you do. Please let them see you in me.'

After the meal I hovered in the kitchen to make some small talk with Mum as she fussed and busied herself over the dishes. Finally she made a tray of hot drinks and carried them through to the lounge where Dad and the girls were sitting watching the TV. I sensed that the moment had come.

There was an awkward silence as I asked if they minded if I switched the set off for a few minutes, because there was something very important that I wanted to tell them all. They shuffled and twisted as I pulled up a chair facing them and, breathing a silent prayer for God's help, brought them up to date with all that had happened.

'First of all I want to say that I'm ashamed for so long having been the worst son you could wish for. I've hurt and embarrassed you, and I've dragged the family name through the mud. I know that I have been a disgrace to you all,' I said quietly, watching their faces.

'But I want you to know that three-and-a-half months ago I became a Christian. I began a personal relationship with Jesus Christ. I asked him into my life, and he forgave me for all the wrong I'd done. He lives in my heart right now, and he's completely changing my life. I want to live for him for the rest of my life.'

It had been so important to me to communicate the passion I held that it had all come out in a bit of a rush, and my story was received with an uncomfortable silence. We'd never been a family for sharing our emotions — except for anger maybe – and I'd just opened my heart in a completely new way.

Mum broke the silence. 'Johnny, it's wonderful to have you home again, son, but I don't understand. You've always been a Christian. I'm glad that you've decided to calm down a bit now, but....' Her words trailed away in confusion.

'Mum, it's not a matter of that,' I replied desperately. 'It's really that God's changed my life. Jesus has set me free. He's made me a new person.'

Trish broke the moment by getting up, walking over and turning the television on again, and the strained silence was washed away in the dialogue of another soap opera.

Leaving them to watch, I slipped out of the room and upstairs to my old bedroom. Safely inside, with the door closed, I fell to my knees beside the bed and began to pray for them, individually and by name, pleading with God to reveal himself to them through his Holy Spirit, in the same dramatic way that he had broken into my life. Although I was discouraged, I was sure deep inside that it was only a matter of time.

Peter Gruschka had been given permission to stay in Sarah and Jenny's flat while they were away. It was only a few hundred yards away, so we'd meet up every morning to spend a couple of hours praying together and reading the Bible. These were important times for me, in which I'd draw heavily on his knowledge and guidance, and feel myself growing stronger and stronger in my love for God. Even before I met with Peter I would often have spent an hour or more praying on my own. I'd rise early before there was any other sound in the house, make myself a large mug of coffee, and settle myself down with the Bible. I still couldn't get enough of it. In the afternoons and evenings I'd often wrap up in a heavy coat and slip down to the other end of our road, where there was open land that led down to the edge of the River Trent. I'd walk up and down alone, singing under my breath and praying long and hard for my family, my old friends and for my future. If the occasional cyclist or dog-walker passing by looked strangely at me as I apparently muttered to myself, I didn't care. I was so happy.

I'd determined from the moment I got home that I'd reinforce the change in my character by my attitude. It wouldn't be hard; I'd been such a poor advert for a son previously that any change for the better would be marked. In addition to being up early, I'd be home most evenings if I wasn't meeting Peter or going for a prayer walk. I never went down to the pub as I had in the old days, but would prefer to stay in and read quietly in my room, or watch TV with the rest of the family. And, quietly, privately, I continued to beg God to touch the rest of my family powerfully, personally.

Joan was first. It was the first full Sunday I'd been home, and the rest of the family was out of the house. Joan was at home with her baby son, Sean. A former air hostess, Joan had gone through a number of relationships before getting engaged to be married. Then she'd become pregnant and the plans had fallen through. She had come home to have the baby and was now trying to pick up the pieces of her life. But she was struggling. Tranquillisers and constant cigarettes were the only things that seemed to get her through the day. It hurt me to see the older sister I'd always resented as a tough, self-possessed person, now so vulnerable and needy.

With the house quiet, I sat down with her and began to tell her in a little more detail all that had happened to me. She seemed interested, so I pressed on, telling her how Jesus wanted to transform people's lives if only they would let him. He could forgive them all the wrong things they had done, take away the hurts, and fill them with a peace and a joy and a hope that was almost beyond belief. I knew, because it had happened to me.

As I talked, she suddenly burst out: 'I know it's all true! When you sat us all down the other night and began to speak I just knew that God existed. I don't really know how to explain it, Johnny, but I just knew, deep down, that what you were saying was true. I believe it ... and I know it's what I've been looking for all my life. What should I do?'

I explained to her how she needed to admit all the wrong things she'd done, say she was sorry to God for them, and ask Jesus into her heart as her Lord and Saviour, and that he'd come – no doubt about it. She began to pray, falteringly, along the lines I'd suggested, and as she did she began to weep. She slumped to the floor, crying aloud.

My heart was somersaulting with joy, but I didn't know what to do as she lay on the floor beside me. So I started to pray too, asking God to answer her prayers and give her a new life. I don't know how much time we spent in this way, but eventually Joan's tears dried away. She knelt up with a beautiful smile of peace on her face and began to whisper: 'Thank you, God, thank you. Thank you, Jesus. This is what I've been wanting for so long.'

When she stood up and looked into my eyes, I couldn't believe it. Her face seemed visibly softer already, and it almost appeared to glow. Through the tear-smudged eyes I could see the sparkle of real happiness. We hugged and held each other tight. I buried my head in her shoulder, and murmured: 'Thank you, Father God. Thank you!'

As well as the heaviness that dropped from her features, the anxiety went that afternoon. Joan found out straight away that she no longer needed the tranquillisers or the tobacco to calm her nerves. In the days that followed we began to meet together in my room to read the Bible and pray, and it was wonderful to share my limited knowledge with another young Christian who was as enthusiastic and hungry to learn as I had been. We told the rest of the family what had happened, but they seemed to dismiss it all as a bit of emotional nothingness; everything would be back to normal again after I'd been home a few weeks and things had settled down a bit.

Trish didn't really seem to understand what was going on. As a fashion- and music-conscious young teenager, she thought that her older brother and sister were just going through a religious phase; that it was something they would come out of. I sensed that she was keeping a quiet eye on me, watching secretly to see if I made any mistakes.

A few weeks later, though, she agreed to go to an evangelistic rally at Nottingham's Albert Hall. The speaker was Nicky Cruz, the tough New York gang leader who'd been saved through the remarkable ministry of David Wilkerson. His story had been told in *The Cross and the Switchblade*, and I was keen to hear the man whose life in so many ways seemed to mirror my own.

Joan, Peter and I went along that night, but we somehow got separated from Trish and her young friends. We didn't see her again until much later, on the way home. She was sitting a few seats forward on the top deck of the bus, and when I called her name, she turned round – and flashed me a broad, excited grin. I knew that she, too, had met Jesus. 'Thank you, thank you, thank you,' I softly repeated all the way home.

As the weeks went by and the home Bible study group grew to three strong, my parents seemed to relax a little. They didn't like to talk too much about what was happening in a direct way, but they sensed that it was bringing peace, closeness and happiness to their children, so they were happy enough. Not everyone felt the same. One night Mum came home after seeing relatives, and it was evident that there had been harsh words exchanged about the strange new religion I was bringing into the house — this new kind of faith. What about the Catholic church? Mum was extremely agitated, wringing her hands and chewing her lip. She took her coat off, walked into the room and promptly burst into tears.

'My life's falling apart. I'm losing all my children and we're falling out. What's happening here? I just don't know what's going on, any more. You've got to help me, John,' she said.

I looked up at her, full of pain for her. 'I can't, Mum. Nobody can. Only Jesus.'

'I want to be like you and the girls. How do I get what you've got in your lives?'

'You've got to invite Jesus into your heart, Mum. That's all. Just turn to Jesus.'

Collapsing into the chair she said that she wanted to, straight away. I went over and put my arm around her and led her in a brief prayer, asking Jesus to forgive her for where she had failed and come into her life. As we finished, she jumped up suddenly. 'It's gone, son, it's gone. The burden has gone. All the guilt's gone; I feel lighter!'

Mum stopped drinking straight away. If Dad felt threatened by this latest transformation in his family, he didn't say so. But by now he was an old man, with only a hint of the iron there had once been. Officially retired, he had a part-time job at a local pub, and spent his time pottering about there or in the back garden. I felt so sorry for him. He seemed trapped inside his own past hardness, and I longed to be able to reach inside. He allowed me to start saying a brief prayer for all of us before meals, and we'd work silently but contentedly together when I'd help him turning over his garden. He didn't say very much, but I could feel that he approved of some of the changes he was seeing. Mum, the girls

and I continued praying that God would touch his
heart.

Another Sunday at home, but so different from many of
the old years. We've just finished lunch after morning
service at church, and there's a quiet, peaceful sort of
contentment about the house. Over the past months,
Mum, Joan, Trish and I have grown close in a special
way that I still thank God for. It's like he's helping us to
make up for all the time we've lost in the past.

The door goes in the kitchen, and I know it's Dad
back from his Sunday drinks down at the pub. He's
almost timid these days, just a shadow of the man I used
to hate and fear in equal measure. Oh, Dad, how can I
ever get through to you? The thoughts and feelings
tumble together, as I sense God speaking into my heart:
'Go into the kitchen and tell your father the good news
about Jesus Christ.'

It may sound strange, but now I've come to trust this
inner prompting by God's Spirit. So I walk through to
the kitchen where he's sitting on a chair, with his head
slumped in his hands. He seems very old and very tired.
He looks up at me wearily as I come in, and drops his
head again.

'Dad, the Lord has told me to come in and share the
gospel with you. And this is the word of God to you. It's
the first three verses of Isaiah 61.' And I read: 'The
Spirit of the Lord ... has anointed me to preach good
news to the poor ... to bind up the broken-hearted, to
proclaim freedom for the captives ... .'

I close my Bible and looking straight over at him
begin to talk freely and effortlessly. For almost ten
minutes I tell him boldly about the good news of Jesus,
and the hope he offers. There is a special sense of
authority and power, and I'm raising my voice as though
I'm addressing a crowd of hundreds. Yet Dad sits, head
down, just a few feet away – almost as though he doesn't
hear me.

But as I finish, he looks up slowly. There are tears in his eyes and it's the first time I've seen him weep without a bottle in his hand. These are real tears, and something breaks inside me. Dad drops to his knees from the chair, and I rush forward, kneeling down beside him on the lino and putting my arms around him. It feels good.

'Son, what shall I do to be saved?' he croaks.

'Dad, ask Jesus into your heart. Here, like this . . .' and we stumble through a short prayer together and spend a long time just holding on to each other.

Putting my broken family relationships right was something I began work on the moment I arrived back in Nottingham. But there were many other loose ends that needed knotting up so that they didn't entangle me in my new life. In addition to praying for God to work in my family, each morning when Peter and I met together we would ask for help in knowing the way ahead for all the other things that still had to be sorted out.

Within a few days of my return, our old gang was reunited. The other three had all found their way back to Nottingham during the previous weeks when I'd stayed on The Ark, and had, like me, given themselves up to the police with the express intention of putting things straight. With all we had gone through together we were still fairly close, but those crossroads days in Amsterdam had driven something of a wedge between us. Gary had also committed his life to Christ, and was following his own plan for sorting his life out. Mac told me shortly before he left The Ark that he believed all that the people there said about God, but he just didn't want to know. Alan had left in a hurry one night, after failing to persuade me to go with him.

Back in Nottingham we continued to meet together for the first few weeks after my return, and we'd study the Bible with Peter, in effect picking up on the searching, discussing and exploring that had been a feature of

The Ark's life. I was distressed by Alan's apparent continued scepticism; after all, he and I had been closest in the gang. He had been the one who had ultimately focused my search for meaning in life to the spiritual realm, through which I had finally found what I was looking for. Now I was anxious that he should make the same discovery, and yet for all the hours we reasoned and talked, he didn't seem to be getting any closer.

Not long after getting back, he found work as a lorry driver, and as I hadn't sorted out a job in the early days I would often accompany him in the cab to continue our discussions. One day, driving back to Nottingham from Leicester, I became so frustrated with his apparent inability or unwillingness to accept what was clearly staring him in the face that I found there were, after all, limits to my new-found patience.

I turned to him and told him: 'Alan, we've talked enough now. That's it. Give your heart to Jesus, man. Come on – you know it's all true! Don't be stubborn. Let's just do it. This is too important to waste any more time over!'

It was an outburst of deep concern, but I wasn't sure if maybe I'd pushed him too hard. It was all quiet for a moment, and then he looked over at me and said quietly: 'OK, John, let's do it.'

Alan pulled off the road into a countryside lane, and drove up to the end a hundred yards or so away from where the heavy traffic rolled past. Switching off the engine he bowed his head over the steering wheel, and I led him in a short prayer of confession and invitation to Jesus. Sitting up again, he beamed, jumped down from the cab and began to shout at the top of his voice: 'It's really true, John! I believe it, you know!'

He fell to his knees on the grass as I climbed down to join him. 'Look at the trees!' he shouted happily as the tears started to fall. 'God made them, didn't he? God really made them! Oh, it's fantastic!' His stubbornness and fear had finally been swept away, and in their place was a bubbly joy.

Looming on the horizon was our forthcoming trial. We'd been bailed to appear at Nottingham Crown Court some five months after my return. It gave us strength and encouragement to think that we were all facing this thing together. We'd already been warned that the charge – conspiracy to defraud – was particularly serious. And having previous offences, it was almost certain that we would be sent to prison, despite our willingness to help the police as much as we could.

When I'd been interviewed by detectives on arriving back in England, they hadn't asked me if I had committed any other offences: I would have admitted it if they had. This left a catalogue of outstanding incidents still to be dealt with. One of the Bible passages that made a deep impression on me during this time was when Zacchaeus the tax collector became a disciple of Jesus. He immediately said that he wanted to repay all the debts he had—put right all the wrongs. It was a free expression of his gratitude to God. I felt the same, and Peter and I talked and prayed about the best way of going about it.

Finally, one morning, after we had spent an hour or so in prayer I sat down with pen and paper to make a list of all those I had stolen from. There was the jeweller's shop where I'd made my smash and grab; the bank where I'd run up a large illegal overdraft; the insurance companies I'd conned out of bogus sick pay while self-employed; a fashion shop where I'd obtained clothes on forged credit, the takings I'd pocketed secretly at the Crazy Horse Saloon and the Swiss hotel ... the list went on and on.

Then I turned to all those individuals I'd hurt – physically and emotionally. I tried to remember all the names of the people I'd battered and bruised – that included women. Like the evening a girl in a pub had made a rude remark when I bumped into her, and I'd punched her in the face, giving her a black eye. I jotted down the names, too, of the women I had wronged through my selfish relationships. Sharon's name came first.

My wrist started to ache, but I continued to scribble away. We'd prayed that God would help me to remember every last small matter, and other incidents came to mind. The money that I owed on tax from my self-employed days, the muggings and car thefts.

At last, it was finished. I looked at the lengthy list wondering if I could really go through with all this. How blind I'd been! Remembering had been the easy part ... now I had to *do* something with this catalogue of selfishness.

13

Back on the Streets

I'd returned to Nottingham riding so high on being a Christian that I couldn't wait to get out and tell everyone what had happened, even though I was a bit nervous about how I'd go about it. Much of my prayer time concentrated on asking God to help me share in the right ways the incredible good news I'd discovered. And it turned out that there were a number of different avenues to explore.

Having been a part of Nottingham's low scene, word soon seemed to have got round that 'Johnny's back and he's got religion'. I found that most of the old faces I came across knew that something had happened in Amsterdam, and that I was different, or at least claiming to be. They treated me warily, although whenever I got the chance I made stumbling attempts to tell them some of what had been going on inside me since that tearful night on The Ark. One night I drifted into the Flying Horse looking for Cupe. He was one of the city's most well-known hard men, and a man I had really admired.

The Flying Horse was as smokey and noisy as ever, and squinting through the haze I spotted him in a corner with a crowd of friends. They were laughing and drinking freely, and when I went over to their tables, there were some knowing nods and glances in my direction. Undeterred I sat down next to Cupe and said hello.

'Now then, Johnny, how's it going?' he asked brightly.

'Great, Cupe, great,' I replied. 'Maybe you've heard. I've become a Christian.'

'Yeah, that's right. Word's got round. What's it all about, then, youth?'

As he spoke I thought I detected some genuine interest beneath the brusque, rough-and-ready exterior. I began to tell him, hesitantly, about all that I'd been through, and as I did he turned to his drinking mates with a wave of his hand and snapped: 'Quieten down, will you! We're trying to talk here.' They turned to their drinks and we spent twenty minutes or so together, Cupe seeming to hang with interest on my account. Then I said that I'd got something for him, and reached inside my coat pocket for the spare copy of Nicky Cruz's autobiography *Run Baby Run* that I was carrying. Before I'd gone over to Cupe, I'd scribbled a brief greeting in it – 'To Cupe: we've both travelled a hard road' – and prayed for an opportunity to hand it over.

As he looked at the inscription with curiosity, Cupe's eyes filled with tears. I pressed on: 'I want you to know that coming to know Jesus has transformed my life. It's the most wonderful, beautiful thing you can ever imagine. And he can do the same for you.'

Cupe looked up, embarrassed and vulnerable. 'I know, Johnny, I believe it,' he whispered. Pulling himself together, he turned away with a laugh and snapped back to his former self. 'Well, thanks, Johnny, I'll read this some time,' he said, and went to order another drink.

I was a little disappointed that the moment seemed to have passed, but I was delighted that he'd been so keen to listen. It encouraged me to believe that my old friends would want to hear about God if I persisted in prayer and waited for the right moments to speak out. That encounter with Cupe encouraged me to look for other opportunities to explain what had happened in my life.

They came thick and fast the day I set out on my trail

of restitution. Peter and I had decided that it would be good to complete the journey in one day, if possible. So I got up extra early and spent a couple of hours praying and reading the Bible before heading off for my first appointment at the bank. With that successfully behind me, I was heartened for the calls that followed: at the insurance offices, the guild hall, the jeweller's shop, the tailors. . . .

Some of the people I dealt with were businesslike or even a little short with me – although none took up my invitation to call the police. If they had decided to call in the police for a criminal prosecution, my pending Crown Court appearance for conspiracy to defraud would have meant certain jail. And then there were those, like the manager of the local insurance office, who were warmer. He half smiled when I told him about the false sickness benefit claims I'd made while I was self-employed. He'd been unwilling to pay up, and had only done so when I'd become extremely threatening over the phone.

'I never did believe you, you know,' he said. 'So what's all this change of heart about?'

His genuine interest gave me an opportunity to talk longer about my loneliness and insecurity, the desperate hunt for meaning in all the wrong places, and the incredible new life I'd begun since meeting Jesus. I could have gone on for the rest of the day, but he pulled me up short with a laugh. 'I see you've already started trying to convert people, then!' he chuckled.

'That's right,' I answered.

'Well, I think your coming in here and owning up is the most amazing thing that's ever happened to me in all the years that I've been in this business,' he told me with a shake of his head. 'I wish you well!'

When I finally got home that night I added up all the money that I'd promised to repay. It amounted to several thousand pounds, and I didn't have much more than the cost of a bus fare. But I wasn't downhearted. I was sure that God would give me the strength and ability to see it through to the end. I soon found work back on the building sites, and I laboured hard. Each Friday night I'd bring my fat pay packet home, hand some money over to Mum for my keep, and save myself a few coins for travel and the odd cup of coffee. The rest went down to the Post Office with me the following morning and, converted into a series of postal orders, got posted off to meet my debts. Every week's contribution was duly ticked off in a little black book I had bought for the purpose.

I knew that going back onto the sites would be a real test for my new faith, and I was determined to make it clear from day one that I was a Christian. So when lunch break arrived and I headed over to the cabin with my lunch box, I'd already decided what I had to do. We flopped round the table together, and the other guys opened up their flasks and packs of sandwiches. Meanwhile, I purposefully dropped my head to say a silent grace – and stayed in that position slightly longer than usual in case anyone had missed it. Then I looked up again as I opened my lunch box. One of the men opposite, Lenny, was staring at me with a big grin.

'What's all that about then, eh?'

It was just what I'd hoped for. 'I was praying – saying thank you to God for my food.'

'Oh,' Lenny guffawed, 'that's all right, then. I thought you'd slipped into a coma!' I laughed with him, and the ice was broken. They knew where I stood. Over our break he began to ask me further questions about what a Christian was, and I had a great opportunity to tell him about my journey of the past few years. From that time on the men never sneered at me or joked about my faith, as I'd half thought they would. In time, in fact, I found that they'd single me out to have a quiet word with me. They'd want my advice about what they should do about their relationships with women, or to voice their concern about a teenage son going off the rails. A few asked me to pray for them, and I did – along with all those who hadn't asked!

My wish to make exhaustive attempts at paying restitution involved firing off a series of overseas letters to people I'd ripped off on my travels. Not being a great writer I found this particularly difficult, but in due course the replies came back saying there were no hard feelings, and wishing me well. The toughest letter to write was the one I sent locally in Nottingham, however – to Sharon. I figured that it would be wrong of me to seek her out personally. So I told her all that had gone on, as best I could, and asked her to see if she could find her way to forgive me for the dreadful way I'd treated her and ruined her life. I offered to meet up with her if she wanted to, and told her I'd set in motion repayment of all the maintenance that I'd for so long refused to pay.

I never did hear from her, and the silence was painful. But I resolved to pray for her and our daughter – whom I last saw as a six-month-old in a family snapshot – in the hope that one day they may be able to find it in their hearts to forgive me. Not because I deserve it, but because they've found the love and healing and wholeness that Jesus can bring. Perhaps one day.

While I decided it was best not to try to make direct contact with Sharon, I did seek out a number of other women, with whom I'd had fleeting relationships, as I went round my old circle of friends specifically to put right incidents from the past.

I saw one woman in The Flying Horse one night, drinking with a group of friends. I'd had a brief affair with her when her marriage – to a friend of mine – had been breaking up. I went over to her and asked if I could have a private word with her for a moment. She seemed surprised to see me, but stepped out into the hall. It was an awkward moment, and I didn't know where to begin.

'Look, Suzy, you'll probably think I'm crazy,' I said, shifting uncomfortably. 'But I've become a Christian. . . .'

'I know,' she interrupted, looking at me uncertainly. 'I'd heard that you'd gone all religious, like. I hope you're not going to try to lay any of that on me, are you?'

This wasn't going at all as I'd hoped. 'Well, I want to tell you that I'm sorry for having committed adultery with you, and I want to ask you to forgive me if I caused you any hurt.'

She bristled. I'd obviously offended her. Her eyes flashed. 'So what's wrong with a bit of sex on the side?'

'Well, I'm a Christian, and I believe it's wrong to have sex with someone if you're not married.'

'Well I don't,' she almost shouted as she turned on her heels and walked off. 'I'm not sorry, and as far as I'm concerned there's nothing to forgive, so you can just get lost with all your Holy Joe stuff, mister.'

I was glad it was over. Heading home that night I felt wounded and tender, but I knew that I'd tried to do the right thing.

My efforts to tell others about Jesus were limited to conversations with one or two people at a time – usually against the backdrop of a noisy bar – until the day came for us to present ourselves for trial. Mac, Gary, Alan and I had all pleaded guilty to the offence, and had been delighted to find a solicitor who volunteered to take us on. He was from the congregation of the small evangelical church we'd begun to attend.

We arrived at the guild hall, where the Crown Court was sitting, having prayed for the strength to accept God's will that day. I'd already been day-dreaming about how I'd start a prison Bible study if the worst came to the worst and I was jailed. I was determined that whatever the outcome, I'd make it count for God. But we were greeted by an excited solicitor who told us: 'God is already at work – they've dropped the conspiracy charges!'

It was thrilling. This massively reduced the seriousness of the offence in the eyes of the law. When we finally stepped into the dock, we all pleaded 'guilty' and waited as the prosecuting officials told our story. Then our defence representative told how we'd given ourselves up to help the police clear the matter up, and how our experiences on The Ark had changed our lives radically. Within a matter of minutes we were walking free with fines, costs – and an eighteen-month prison sentence suspended for two years! We hugged each other and our families and thanked God for giving us our freedom. And the next day the story of our transformation – which the judge had said was so remarkable that it had prompted him to sentence us as first-time offenders, even though we had previous convictions – was recounted in the city's evening paper for all to see.

The evangelical church through which we'd found our legal help had been marvellous to us. They were a fairly traditional, middle-class congregation, but if they'd been shocked by this small group of enthusiastic, young people who had appeared in their midst, then they had done their very best to disguise it. We felt accepted straight away, and loved to attend all the meetings; the Sunday services, the mid-week prayer and Bible study evenings. As time went by, though, and we continued to make contacts among the old group of friends I'd known – and found a number of them turning to Christ – we began to feel a little uncomfortable. My heart was bursting for people who were as lost as I had been to find Jesus; yet evangelism seemed to have a low priority in the church's life.

Eventually a group of us began meeting in Sarah and Jenny's flat. They'd returned from The Ark turned upside down after their own encounters with God. In time they'd introduced us to Sarah's brother, Jamie, a young tailor, whom we had befriended. He'd become a Christian at the evangelical church, and was soon leading the informal fellowship meetings in the flat, with me.

Before we knew it we were thirty or more young people
there each week; new Christians converted through our
circle of contacts, or others from churches in the area
looking for more dynamism and vibrancy in their walk
with God. Although it was still only a few months since
I'd become a Christian, God seemed to equip me in a
special way and I was able to pass on all the teaching I'd
absorbed during my intensive time of study on The Ark.
Our mid-week meetings were alive with the presence of
God, as the Holy Spirit would move powerfully and yet
at the same time gently among us. There would be tears,
laughter, prayer and praise in an easy-going, open way
that soon made newcomers feel at ease.

After one particularly moving time of praise and
worship, I suggested that we should take this meeting
out into the open air. After all, what would God do if
non-Christians were around to witness it all? The others
agreed, so one Sunday afternoon we headed down into
the centre of Nottingham, to the square in front of the
guild hall.

Nervously we tuned up our guitars, picked up our
maraccas and bongos, and began to sing praises to
God, slipping from one short, happy song to another.
Within a few minutes we'd attracted a sizable crowd of
afternoon strollers who watched and listened. After
about twenty minutes we stopped and tried to engage
some of the onlookers in conversation, but it was a toss-
up as to who was more ill at ease about it all – them or
us. So we made our way home, happy at the way things
had gone, but frustrated that they hadn't been even
better.

We repeated this pattern for a few weekends until at
the end of one singing session I was approached by
Ansell. He was a short, wiry miner, originally from
Jamaica, who usually occupied the square before we did.
Dressed in his smartest suit, he stood on top of a
concrete post and, holding a Bible to his chest, shouted
out how people need God in their lives. I'd seen him in

action a couple of times when we'd arrived early to set up, and I'd been at once impressed by his bravery and intimidated by the negative reaction of some of those listening.

This particular Sunday Ansell stayed on to listen to us sing, and afterwards singled me out. He smiled and thanked us for singing about Jesus so freely. I was pleased. 'But, you know,' he added seriously, 'you've got to preach the gospel. You've got to tell them how Jesus can save them. You won't see anyone converted simply by your singing alone. You've got to tell them the good news!'

Deep down I knew he was right, but I was alarmed at the prospect. What would people think if we did what Ansell did? Would they laugh at us in the same way? Were any of us brave enough? At that week's Tuesday meeting we all talked and prayed about what he had said – and we agreed that he was right. We had to stand up and speak out next Sunday. The only question was, who?

Everyone's eyes turned in my direction.

The last of our songs is ringing round the square, and I realise that the moment has come. I'm terrified and breathe a silent prayer for help as I step up on top of a wooden bench and look out towards the crowd that has gathered to hear us singing and clapping.

I'm not really sure what I'm going to say, but it's too late to back out now, so I raise my hand in a gesture of acknowledgement and open my mouth. As I do I'm aware of a flood of confidence surging through my body, rising up from my feet and welling into my heart – and out through my mouth. My mind's suddenly racing with thoughts and ideas, and the words come out unexpectedly. They're not hesitant or timid, but bold and confident. It doesn't sound like me at all!

'D'you know,' I begin, 'I never used to be up this time

on a Sunday! I used to stagger across this square dead
drunk most weekends, and if I'd seen somebody doing
what I'm doing now, I'd have thought that he was
completely barmy!' I pause and smile, and see some of
the crowd turn away. But others smile back and look
interested. I continue.

'You see that jeweller's shop just down the road,
there? I broke into that one night . . . smash and
grab. Got caught by the police a bit further up the street.
I used to get into fights in that pub there, too . . .' and
I begin to tell my story of drinking and fighting and
sex and drugs and violence and lostness. And Jesus. The
words spill out almost effortlessly, and the fear has gone
completely. In its place is a keen thrill I've never known
before.

Finally I've come full circle. 'And so that's why I'm
here today with some of my friends. We're going to be
staying here for a bit yet, so if you want to know any
more, just come and have a chat with us. Thank you.'
And I step down, tingling with excitement and satisfaction. Ansell's right – there's power in preaching the
gospel. I for one feel as though I've just been plugged
into the mains. This is something I'm going to want to
do again and again. . . .

Encouraged by the warm response our first public
preaching received, other members of the group wanted
to try it over the next few weeks. I was keen to give
them an opportunity so long as I was able to speak
again as well! I found myself looking forward to
the Sunday afternoon meetings with great longing.
I'd still be nervous when the afternoon finally arrived,
but once I stood up and opened my mouth I sensed God
filling me with authority, clarity and confidence, and
I enjoyed telling the passers-by about Jesus' tremendous
love.

If any of those who stopped to listen wanted to talk
further, we would sit down with them for the afternoon,

or invite them along to our Tuesday night meeting. And
soon we found that there were a number of new
Christians through our street meetings. Our weekly
numbers grew to over forty as God's love was shared
with family, friends and acquaintances, and they
responded. Wherever possible we tried to encourage
newcomers to find their way through to local churches,
but many felt that the closeness of God they felt in our
Tuesday meetings wasn't there at some of the more
formal Sunday services they attended.

As winter drew nearer, the cold weather meant that
people were less keen to stand and listen to us – and,
indeed, we were less enthusiastic about being there – so
we turned more to prayer and Bible study. Within a
matter of a few months we had developed a growing
fellowship, comprising mostly young and new Christians.
I felt confident that God had enabled me to cope with
all the demands this made up to now – I certainly knew
that I didn't have the resources within myself – but
I began to worry about future direction. I didn't
think our young leadership could run things for ever
this way.

I'd kept in touch with The Ark over the months,
advising them of my spiritual growth and all that was
happening in a series of lengthy letters. I'd also asked
them to pray about our fellowship's situation when, in a
reply, Floyd McClung suggested that a couple from The
Ark should perhaps come over to England to lend some
experienced hands to the scene. We were delighted, and
in due course welcomed Paul and Mary Miller, an
American couple who had become Christians while
following the hippy trail in India, and had been key
workers at The Ark for a couple of years.

It was a brave move on their part. They arrived in
grey, cold Nottingham knowing little about what they
faced, and found themselves a small bedsit. I relin-
quished formal leadership of the fellowship and handed
the responsibility over to Paul, acting as his assistant

along with Jamie. Under the Millers' direction and gentle guidance, the fellowship continued to flourish and grow – both in numbers and in the knowledge of God's love and power in our lives.

The days were busy, bursting with an ever-deepening love for God and this wonderful, exciting new life he had given me. I was so happy with our newly-united family; the opportunities to talk about God at work on the sites; the debts being paid off and the new things we were all learning in the fellowship. Life seemed as full as it could possibly be.

There was only one shadow. One day I was laying bricks on a housing scheme down in the old Meadows part of the town – in fact just across the street from where we'd lived and been attacked by the cousin with the knife. It was early morning, and I'd not been going long when my heart spasmed. I went cold inside. 'Home, I've got to get home,' I told myself. I knew it was God prompting me. I threw my tools into my bag, thrust them back into the store shed and leaped over the wall to run off to the bus stop, shouting back over my shoulder that I'd got to go home suddenly.

When I got back, I was met at the door by a distraught Trish. 'It's Dad, John. There's been an accident. ...'

Poor Dad. He'd been struck by a bus down in the town, and had suffered serious head injuries in the fall. He was in the intensive care unit down at the hospital. Joan, Mum and I fell into each other's arms and prayed for God's help to be strong.

Two days later Dad died without regaining consciousness, and we all wept together. We'd only been close as a family for a few short months. It almost seemed cruel. And yet through our grief of bereavement, we could see a test of our faith. We knew that if we weren't careful we could easily become negative towards God for having allowed this tragedy to happen. But as we wept and mourned and comforted each other, we agreed that we could trust God. Though we didn't understand fully, we knew there was a reason for the way things had turned out. Our tears of grief were mixed with thankfulness for God's goodness to us in allowing us the days we had enjoyed together as a family, in him. Gradually we came to see how different it was to face death with God in our lives. Even in the sadness, there was a real sense of hope for the future.

14

Plenty to Learn

There were three high points to my week; each of them a far cry from the sort of pastimes I'd looked forward to in former days. There were Tuesday evenings, when we'd come together in the girls' small flat to praise God and learn more about him. I often used to smile when I thought back to how, a matter of months earlier, I'd been living in a small bedsit in a room upstairs, frightened of living and scared of dying. Now life and death thrilled and consumed me. Every day was an adventure in living for Jesus, and the prospect of being with him for ever was almost too much to contemplate.

Saturday mornings were special, too. It gave me a great sense of satisfaction to bundle off my small pile of payments in the post. I enjoyed knowing that I'd put in another week's hard work, and that another entry could be made in my account book: a visible record of my determination to put right, with God's help, all that I could of the old days.

But most of all I loved Sunday afternoons, when we'd gather to sing and preach in the town centre. That marvellous buzz of adrenalin and excitement that had charged through me the first time I stood up, never failed to return every time I took my turn talking to the crowds. I knew that this was what I wanted to spend the rest of my life doing, and as soon as I'd paid off my final debts, I would commit myself to full-time evangelism out in the open air. For a short period I actually stopped work and joined Paul in a daily programme of street preaching near to Nottingham's main shopping precinct. We'd spend the morning praying together and the afternoon taking turns to preach and talk with shoppers and passers-by who paused to listen and chat. This 'work experience' time only whetted my appetite further, and I returned to the building sites more determined than ever to work my way through my repayments as swiftly as possible and get into full-time ministry as quickly as I could.

A way of helping things along seemed to pop up when I came across an advertisement for bricklayers wanted in Germany. I'd been working hard and steadily in Nottingham for around two-and-a-half years, and while I'd made a large dent in my debts there was still a frustratingly long way to go. But the firm seeking brickies were offering money well over the odds found in England – perhaps here was the route God was providing for me.

I calculated that if I worked flat out for six weeks or so then I could come home with all the money I needed; as against the year or more it would take me at British rates. So I followed the offer up, got myself an interview and almost before I knew it found myself travelling out to the site, a small German town not far from the Dutch border. I was to be picked up at the station by the guy in charge of the building programme, the English manager of a small firm.

When I arrived I found myself being met along with two or three other British brickies who were making the trip. Memories of my Canadian travels came back to me, but I shook them off.

The last time I'd been trying to master my own destiny – and failed abysmally; this time I knew God was firmly in control. Our first port of call was the nearest pub, where the other men immediately ordered a couple of beers each. My request for a Coke raised their eyebrows, and I was able to spend a few minutes telling them about why I'd turned my back on drinking.

After a while the site manager offered to take me over to the hotel in which I was to be accommodated, to sort out the final few details. On the way, in the car, I asked him about what arrangements had been made to sort out my tax payments.

He laughed and looked over at me.

'What's so funny?'

'You've got to be kidding. We don't pay tax!'

'What do you mean?' I asked. All was not as I had expected, obviously.

'It's cash in hand. No tax, no questions. In fact, nobody really knows that we're over here on the job. We're sub-contracted out by somebody else back home.'

My heart sank. I hadn't even got as far as unpacking my bags, and it seemed like the whole arrangement was falling apart. 'You mean it's black money, then?'

'Well, yeah, if you want to call it that,' he replied, shifting uncomfortably in his seat. 'But everyone does it, you know, it's all accepted.'

'Maybe,' I cut in. 'But not for me. One of the reasons I'm here for the job is to pay off a load of money that I owe the taxman! I can't work on this basis. I'll have to go back home.'

The driver looked at me with a mixture of annoyance and amazement. 'You've got to be kidding! That's good money down the drain. What are you, some kind of weirdo, or something?'

'I'm a Christian,' I explained. 'I've given my life to Jesus, and he wouldn't want me to do this. I'm sorry.'

My driver turned the car around, and we headed back to the station. It was an uncomfortable few minutes' drive, and he spent the time trying to justify his actions by explaining how it was all part of the system; nobody expected you to do differently. Nobody really lost out; the government wouldn't miss a few hundred pounds. I didn't answer.

Standing back outside the station, with my bag over

my shoulder, I sagged. In just a couple of hours my carefully-made plans seemed to have been dashed. I was confused and a bit disappointed. I knew that God had some sense in all of this, somewhere, but right then it was beyond me. I needed some time and space to think and pray it through so that I could see what he was doing. I decided to travel over the border and back to Holland.

My destination was Heidebeek, a picturesque little hamlet about sixty miles to the north of Amsterdam. Since I'd left The Ark, they had become part of Youth With a Mission, an international missionary organisation with operations all over the world. They had also expanded their work in Holland, keeping The Ark going while opening a training base out in the Dutch countryside.

Joan had contacted them some months after my homecoming, and with her toddler son had gone out to Holland. There she'd gone through the new Discipleship Training School in which young Christians were given a thorough grounding in their faith, before going into full-time service of one kind or another. Joan had then stayed on to become part of a ministry house in Epe, near Heidebeek. She and Sean loved the environment – the love of the people and the beauty of the countryside setting made it a real haven of peace. I'd been impressed by what I'd seen in the two previous brief visits that I had made.

So I arrived unexpectedly, but to a warm welcome. And later, over coffee with Floyd McClung – renewing our friendship with smiles and hugs – I told him about my hopes and dreams, and how they all seemed to have collapsed. He looked at me in his thoughtful, 'I've-got-an-idea-coming' way.

'John, why don't you just stay here and go through our Discipleship Training School? We've got one starting next week.'

I knew from the past that Floyd had a knack of

making the most outrageous ideas seem matter-of-fact, but this one seemed too way out – even for me. I had my near-future mapped out, and studying the Bible in the middle of a Dutch forest had no part in it. I had to work because I had to pay my debts. I spluttered a dismissive answer, tailing off with: '... and I've not finished paying restitution, either.'

Floyd didn't seem perturbed by my objections. He smiled. 'Well, why don't you just go away and pray about it, and ask the Lord if this is right or not? If it is, then he'll provide for you, John.'

I was certain that I already knew what the answer was, but my respect for this gentle-spoken, smiling American packed me off praying. And I had to admit that I'd become so determined to do what God wanted me to, that I'd failed to recognise that he wanted to help.

During my prayers my mind was filled with a simple picture. I saw a series of different doors that seemed to represent the ways open to me, avenues I could explore to pay back all the hundreds of pounds that I still owed. And as I gazed at them, one by one they closed. Firmly. At last there was only one door still open, tucked away at the side of my mind's eye, and above it was one word ... Heidebeek. The door was ajar, and flooding through and round the gap was a bright, welcoming light. It seemed like warm sunlight, the sort you just want to go and throw yourself into. That's how I felt, and I realised that God was speaking clearly to me: he did want me to go through the DTS (Discipleship Training School). And if I left to go home again, I'd be acting disobediently.

I didn't understand, but I knew what I had to do. When I found Floyd I told him: 'You're right. I've prayed about it, and I believe that the Lord wants me to stay here.'

It's a bright, sunny morning, and the sun filters through

the trees in a haze of glorious colours. The woods smell
fresh and crisp, and the only sound comes from the few
farm animals grazing nearby. It's a beautiful morning a
world away from my early starts on a Nottingham
building site, and I almost pinch myself again to make
sure that it's real. Yes, I'm still here!

As I walk over to the main building, where the DTS
classes are due to start soon, I wonder again at the turn
of events. I realise that I'd made the mistake of narrow-
ing down God's plan for me into a specific pathway. I'd
decided that there was only one way to do what he
expected of me – and that was working my debts off.
Now I'm beginning to understand that there may be
other possibilities. I've still got a long way to go to clear
my outstanding monies, and I've got nothing to meet
the fees of this course – only a few pounds in my pocket.
So something beyond my best efforts is needed.

I'm idling these thoughts over in my mind as I check
my post. My phone call home had caused excited
bewilderment, and I'm anticipating some letters from
the rest of the family. Nothing there, though – except
one envelope. There's no stamp on it, though, so it's not
come through the mail. I slit it open ... and pull out
sixty pounds in folded notes. Tucked in the middle is a
scrap of paper with just two words on it, 'With love.'

It takes a moment or two to sink in, and then the tears
are stinging my eyes. I'm so moved by the quiet, loving
kindness of whoever has left this gift. But even more,
I'm overwhelmed by the love of the God who has
prompted them to do this. For me.

I whoop and speed off down the hallway to tell what's
happened. And as I go I realise that I'm learning
another deep lesson in my new life. I see how my
determination to do the right thing in clearing my debts
had almost become a matter of pride. *I* was going to do
it. *I* was going to put things right.

Then I see that God's saying: 'No, not that way, John.
I've forgiven you. I love you. You don't have to try to

earn that love through your repayments. Thank you for your commitment to doing what you should – but now I want to meet you halfway.'

The envelopes were there week by week as the DTS continued. Sometimes ten pounds, sometimes thirty, once as much as 200. Always neat and tidy; always anonymous, but for a note of love or encouragement. And always enough to enable me to continue my repayments, pay the school fees and leave a little left over to buy a cup of coffee.

Occasionally I'd feel almost guilty. Why should God provide the money in this way when I could earn it? And then I'd remember that it was because he loved me; because he wanted to; because I could never justify or deserve that love. So I knew I had to stop worrying and look to what else he wanted for me.

As well as learning to trust him for my material needs in a completely new way, I discovered that he wanted me to be a good student. In the nearly three years since I'd become a Christian, I felt that my life had been turned completely upside down. I'd learned a lot in the early days on The Ark, and continued to grow back in Nottingham. Seeing my family and friends come to faith in Jesus too had fuelled my love for him and hunger to tell others.

And yet there was still a lot of refining in me to be done. There was a job of smoothing down and polishing that I only began to see as necessary in the quietness and tranquillity of Heidebeek. In those months of the DTS I came to appreciate that there were still secret hurts and insecurities inside me that had to be dealt with. And through prayer and times of teaching, counselling and ministry with the staff and guest speakers, I knew a deeper, cleansing work of the Holy Spirit in my life.

I still found it quite hard to relate to other people. In the past I'd have hidden that in a bout of drinking or drugs. Now I had to face it and work it through.

Although I was still a bit of a loner, avoiding the snack bar at coffee breaks in preference to being on my own, I could feel changes slowly coming about.

I used to get up early in the morning, before the duties of the day, to enjoy uninterrupted time alone with God. Wrapping a thick blanket around my shoulders, I'd stroll out into the pre-dawn woods, and settle down on the ground by a tree with my Bible at my right hand. There I'd spend a precious couple of hours praying, praising God and mulling over the Bible, as the first rays of the day's sun began to percolate through the branches.

At night I'd devour biographies of Christian pioneers like General Booth, the founder of the Salvation Army, and William Carey, the missionary pathfinder. It used to excite me to think what God had achieved through these men, and I'd fall asleep praying that he might one day use me in a similar way.

The more I grew in my relationship with God, the more clearly I saw that my walk with him depended to a large degree on the choices I made. Not that I directed my steps; he did. But I also had to choose to walk that way. I had to accept the things that he wanted to give me. In a sense God's love could only work as far and as deep in my life as I was prepared to let it. This understanding helped me come to terms with the way our old gang of four had dispersed in the days after our Amsterdam turnaround: we'd pretty much drifted apart after our court appearance.

Mac had never made a commitment. He'd told me back in Nottingham that he believed all that he'd heard and seen on The Ark, but he just wasn't interested.

Gary had followed my tearful steps to Jesus a couple of nights later in Amsterdam. He had returned to Nottingham with a similar desire to tell his old friends what had happened. He went after them in the pubs and clubs, spurning the offer of a beer, settling for a soft drink, and sitting them down to tell them all about Jesus.

In fact he was so anxious to go out and tell others that he couldn't be bothered to waste time, as he saw it, meeting with Peter and me to pray and study the Bible. We began to see less of him; and then, the next time I spotted him in a pub, he was nursing a half-pint of beer. On the next occasion it was a pint – and soon he was back in his old ways. An awkward shrug was the only explanation he could offer when we had an opportunity to talk about all that had gone before.

Alan's situation was probably the most difficult for me to understand. We had been through a lot together. He had been the closest of the other three, and I'd been so excited that day he had prayed for Jesus to come into his life. But then the inner struggle began. 'I know that being a Christian means giving up chasing women, and I just don't know if I can do that,' he told me. My attempts to encourage him that God did have a precious plan for a man and woman—but in the proper context of a committed marriage relationship—just seemed to wash straight over him.

He too turned back. Of the four young men who went searching for God, I seemed to be the only one who found who he was looking for.

At Heidebeek I came to know much more about the wonderful God I served and it only made me even more anxious to get out on the streets to tell others about him.

As the school approached an end, I expected to return to Nottingham to start full-time preaching with Paul and other members of the old fellowship. But Floyd had other plans, and when he asked me to stay on as a staff member, to assist with the next DTS, I knew that it was right to accept.

I'd found that being at Heidebeek was helping me work out a new way of relating to women. Since becoming a Christian I'd been freed from the crude, selfish, disposable view I'd had of the opposite sex from my early teens. But although that twisted attitude had been torn out of my life, in its place was awkwardness and uncertainty. I hadn't had a girlfriend in the last three years. I never looked for one. Instead I'd filled my life with a passion for God, and found him to be all I wanted or needed. Or so I thought.

Gradually I found myself easing up in the company of the female staff members and students. I was able to start treating them like my sisters, and I enjoyed the freedom that brought.

But I was still rocked back on my heels when, one morning, I strolled through the grounds on my prayer time and sensed God speaking to me in that gentle, quiet, assured voice of his: 'John, the girl for you will be in the next school.'

It sounded totally absurd. But I was sure that it had been God speaking.

15
Terry

A few weeks later I realised I'd heard right. Her name was Terry Gray, and I fell hopelessly and wonderfully in love with her at about fifty paces. The moment my eyes fell on her as I scanned the group of new arrivals for the next DTS gathering in the main hall, I knew that my life would never be the same again. One glance set off a chain of reactions that had me reeling inside. My heart started to race.

Self-consciously I made to walk away, as though I had an important errand elsewhere. I was sure that everyone could see my cheeks flushing, and I was horribly uncomfortable with the feelings churning around inside me. I was still busy working through what it meant to be a new man in Christ, and I'd committed my life to telling others about him out on the streets. Falling in love with a girl at first sight just didn't fit in with my plans; and it hardly smacked of the spiritual maturity and solid faith I was aching to see grow in my character! Somehow I managed to force down the emotions that were rising within me, and I pulled myself back together again before the newcomers were introduced to the staff.

Our role was to go through the classes with the students, encouraging them to work through and apply to their own lives the biblical teaching on the character of God and discipleship. In addition, we were there to support and befriend them, and generally ensure that their days at DTS were a time of personal growth, while laying foundations for future service. To help pay my way there, I was also in charge of all the maintenance programmes at Heidebeek – everything from changing a light bulb to laying a new foundation for a service road. If it needed repairing or making, it was my job to see that it happened.

Despite my thirst for Bible knowledge, and the rich discoveries I'd made during my time in discipleship training, I found it hard to apply myself this second time around. I struggled to concentrate, like holding a rudder to the right course in a strong wind, but my thoughts kept veering away. They would be followed by my eyes when I'd turn casually to sneak a quick glance at the young woman who had thrown me into a secret turmoil.

Concerned to make sure that no one else picked up the inner confusion I was experiencing, I made a point of avoiding any real contact with her, other than in the odd times when I'd sit and share a coffee in a group. I continued to carve myself away for long hours alone with God, reading the Bible or Christian biographies. But I also ran through my mind the few things I'd managed to glean about her from overhearing the odd conversation.

She was twenty-one, and came from a respectable, middle-class home in the American South. Terry had become a Christian as a teenager, and felt that she was called to missionary service in Europe at sixteen. A French and Bible student, she had gone on a summer ministry trip with Wheaton College in Europe when she'd met Floyd McClung during a brief stop-over on The Ark, and he had told her about a YWAM community to be opened along similar lines in France. Now she was at Heidebeek preparing to join the staff at this new centre.

These details were in addition to all that I had been able to observe. Trim, with long auburn hair parted down the middle, dark brown eyes and a ready smile, her personality was equally attractive. I soon realised that Terry was a popular figure with her open, easy-going nature and warm sense of humour. I'd often hear her bright peal of laughter from a group of students sitting together talking, or playing board games in the evening.

It was paralysing. The few times we did speak I felt tongue-tied and clumsy, and was sure that she had dismissed me as some kind of awkward schoolboy. And secretly I told myself that I was crazy to feel the way I did about someone I hardly knew – particularly in the light of our past. She was a nice American girl from a good background, and had grown from attending church to a powerful, personal walk with God without so much as a hiccup. And here was I; a rough-edged Englishman from the slum area who had tasted most of the forbidden fruits before they had finally turned to ashes in my mouth. Chalk and cheese went together better than we did!

There was another dimension to my struggle, too. One that seemed to call into question everything I'd been aiming for. All I'd dreamed of in serving God seemed close at hand, and now I found it hard to concentrate because I was mooning over an unreachable girl!

I'd been given the go-ahead to try some street evangelism in Amsterdam. The work of The Ark had always been based on what Floyd called 'friendship evangelism'; gentle, caring, low-key and long-term. He had seen too much 'plastic preaching', and believed that many of the young drop-outs with whom he came into contact would be completely turned off by too direct an approach. Instead, The Ark workers set out to win hearts through friendship – and then talk to them about Jesus. And I knew that it worked, because it had drawn me.

But I also knew the powerful urge I had to tell others about Jesus; those who either may not have the opportunity of being befriended over a period of time, or who needed a more direct challenge to their lives. Many

travellers were already disillusioned with life – that's
why they were on the road. But others didn't think there
was anything missing from their lives. They needed to
be challenged. We had seen it work time after time in
Nottingham, and I had grown in confidence and assurance as the weeks went by. I knew that, eventually, it was
what I wanted to do full time.

To this extent, coming to Heidebeek had been like
going through withdrawal. Floyd was delighted to hear
about our experiences in Britain, but he clearly didn't
think them appropriate to Amsterdam or the work
there. Occasionally we'd talk more about it, and I'd ask if
he might let me at least go and try it. He'd listen, discuss
– and say, no, the time wasn't right. It was frustrating,
but I respected Floyd's wisdom and experience, so I'd
accept his decision. Then I went away, prayed again that
God might one day make it possible for me to preach in
the streets of Amsterdam, and waited for another good
opportunity to talk some more about it with Floyd.

I started to make the occasional visit to Amsterdam
with Paul Filler, another DTS staff member with whom
I had grown especially close, and who shared my enthusiasm for the idea of going onto the streets. We'd tour
the city, talking about what it would be like to start a
programme of open-air evangelism, and praying for
God's leading.

One day, as we strolled around, I had a strange
experience. All the faces of the people we passed – old
and cheery, young and angry, foreign and lost – seemed
to be caught, frozen on the back of my mind. It was like
a private slide-show of the lostness of all the people
packed into the city. I felt that God was showing this
private screening to say: 'Look, John, in all the crowds
there are people. And they need to hear about my Son.'

Then, finally, one day, Floyd agreed. I could take a
small team from the school onto the streets!

We began with one-day excursions, when we'd all pile
into a van to drive into the city from Heidebeek. We'd

sing some praise songs in one of the squares, and then I'd preach – just the way we had done in Nottingham. We were pleased with the way things went, and so was Floyd, who had joined us out of curiosity. He suggested we extend the scope of what we were doing. I was thrilled, and set about planning a summer outreach programme for the city. It would be a four-week event, with a small group of us based at one of the campsites on the edge of the city. We'd set up a base there among all the drug addicts and travellers, try some open-air evangelism in the city itself, and invite those interested in learning more to come and spend some time with us at the camp – rather like The Ark under canvas.

After a morning of prayer and praise with the rest of the Heidebeek staff and workers – who had some mixed views on the idea of the outreach – I and my small team headed off for Amsterdam in two crammed vans. Among the group was Terry Gray, who had discovered midway through the DTS that the French community she'd been intending to join was not now going ahead as planned. Instead she proposed to join the YWAM base out at Lausanne, Switzerland, where French-speakers were required. But that left a month to kill – and the Amsterdam outreach seemed like a good idea.

'No sex! No violence! No war!' The words are repeated over and over, like a litany, cutting through the bubble of street chatter and music. A few heads turn to see who's chanting, but many don't. It's not uncommon for people to do their own thing on the bustling streets of the city – this is just another guy overloaded on acid, or maybe speed.

But I sense otherwise. Our first few days working in the open air have gone well. We've sung some lively praise songs as a group, I've stepped up to preach briefly, and we've then split up to try to engage the listeners in further conversation. There has been great interest, and already some of the young people have begun drifting back to our campsite to hear more over coffee or dinner.

I know that this positive start is because of the way the ground has been prepared over the previous weeks. Ever since the go-ahead was given, I've been travelling into the city with a couple of other staff members. We've walked up and down all these streets, past the sex clubs and brothels and cafés selling drugs over the counter and teenagers lying stoned on the pavements, and we've prayed as we walked. We've prayed over all the places to be used as preaching spots, claiming them for God's power and purposes, and in Jesus' name shackling the forces of evil at work there.

So the repetitive cry I hear stirs something within me. This isn't just someone's scrambled gospel; there's more to it. The man is dressed in baggy, flowing clothes, and his eyes have that clouded, faraway look that speaks not of drugs, but of someone whose life is gripped by spirits of evil. Calmly I get him to talk a little more, and he tells us his message comes from his guru. Do we want to go and meet him, too?

Terry decides to come along as well, and the two of us follow eagerly. Only when we're nearly at the top of the stairs, in an old, derelict building a few streets away from the main centre, do I realise that I've misjudged things. Too late, now, though; must just pray for God to protect us.

Stepping into the dusty, dark attic room at the top of the house there's an almost tangible sense of oppressive, heavy evil. Three or four men are lounging around on cushions scattered across the floor, and in the middle is the guru: bare-chested, hard-faced, bearded, suspicious. He views Terry aggressively, speaks to her harshly and fiercely. I sense a wave of hatred, and it all seems to be directed at her. Not waiting to let the situation get out of hand, I smile and tell him what we're doing in the city; how much God loves him, and that he can have a new life in Jesus. A battle is taking place.

Clearly there aren't going to be any takers of an invitation for coffee! I make our excuses, and we back down the stairs, out onto the streets again. It's wonderful to be outside in the clear air again; the weight lifts from us and Terry bursts into tears, burying her head in my shoulder.

I'm annoyed that I hadn't been a bit more discerning before walking into that confrontation. It has obviously shaken her to the roots. The reality of spiritual warfare is new to her; the closeness of the battle between God and his enemy. As I try to comfort her, I'm aware of two things – how I want to make her feel safe for the rest of her life, and how I want to keep fighting the likes of which we've just encountered.

The four weeks were over almost too quickly. We returned to Heidebeek exhausted but happy. We'd made an impact on the streets, quickly learning to adapt what we did and how we did it to the climate of the city and the nature of the laid-back, liberated people who passed through. We'd seen a good number come to Christ through our contacts on the street, or back at the campsite, where at one stage we'd been asked to move on because we were bad for business; the usual drug pedlars who used the place as a base stopped dealing!

My mind was already racing with further possibilities, and how we'd do things bigger and better next time. And I was also wondering what was going to happen with Terry. The last month had only deepened my feelings for her and I couldn't bear the thought of seeing her go off to Switzerland. And yet while I didn't think twice about shouting out in public how I'd become a Christian, I was terrified at the thought of trying to tell her in private what I was thinking.

Finally, after a couple of days skating round each other, it was almost time for her to leave. Just before, she came up to talk about the incident with the demonised man. I explained some more about spiritual warfare, prayer and the supernatural, and we stayed together talking.

There was an awkward silence for a moment, and then Terry said: 'There's something else we need to discuss, isn't there?'

My insides flipped; she knew! Taking a deep breath, and feeling the colour burn my cheeks bright red, I started hesitantly to tell her how I felt. I didn't find it easy, and I stumbled and mumbled my way through. But I managed to say enough, because by the time she did board the bus, Terry and I had agreed to pray about God's leading in our lives.

I was on cloud nine. My thirst for evangelism was being met – Floyd approved of what he'd seen and heard of the outreaches, and was now keen to extend them further – and I'd been able to tell the girl of my dreams that I was in love. Well, at least something along those lines. For the next few weeks I worked in a factory near Heidebeek, raising funds to settle the last of my debts. Those days spent ladling egg powder passed in a happy dream, as I thought about Terry. Even the Scripture memory verse I habitually carried in my shirt pocket couldn't make me concentrate.

I wrote to her two or three times a week; me, the uncommunicative one who'd rarely managed more than a postcard before. I found that I just wanted to sit down with a pen and paper and tell her all about my days: what was happening at Heidebeek; the things God was showing and teaching me; and encouraging her in her walk with him.

The path of true love didn't run smoothly, though. We hit a pothole a few months later when somehow our still-cautious exchanges failed to communicate clearly enough. The upshot was that she spent a day on The Ark when passing through Amsterdam, and took my non-arrival to see her – a visit I didn't realise was expected or possible – as a sign of uninterest. Her letters began to tail off, and mine did in return – my heart sinking at the thought of her not being interested in me any more.

Somehow I managed to bury my disappointment in the business of life at Heidebeek, the prayer walks and plans for further evangelism in Amsterdam. Seven months later I found myself setting off for Venice with a team from Heidebeek. YWAM groups from all over the Continent were to be meeting up at the waterside city for a programme of mass training and outreach. Workers from the Lausanne base were also to be there, Terry among them.

My hands were cold and sweaty and my throat was dry when our coach pulled into the campsite just outside Venice. We were greeted by a welcoming 'orchestra' of other YWAMers, thumping out a symphony of arrival on everything they could lay their hands on: pots, pans, bottles and cans. And there in the middle of the smiling, cheering crowd was Terry. My spirits rose at just seeing her face again, and slumped at the thought of what might have been.

Deliberately I hovered about on the coach while everyone else got off, hoping there would be no need for an awkward encounter. But she was still there, waiting for me, when I finally stepped down. And as I looked at her again, I knew that I was still cartwheelingly in love with her. We exchanged a 'hi' and managed a stiff sort of hug before I had to move on to arrange our accommodation and food. I had plenty to occupy my mind, but other thoughts were in the way. They continued to crowd my thinking over the next few days, even though we didn't see much of each other.

Eventually I plucked up the courage to invite her out for a pizza, and one evening a group of us went into the city. Gingerly we started to explore our feelings again, and my heart soared as I sensed that maybe there was hope to be salvaged here somewhere. In our spare moments we continued to meet, talk, laugh and just enjoy one another's company.

Still being unsure of myself when relating to women, I decided that I needed the wise counsel of an older Christian man. I singled out one I had in mind and poured out my problem. He listened intently, and then advised me: 'John, if you believe that she's the girl for you, then tell her and ask her to pray about it.' It seemed pretty direct to me, but I felt that this man knew what he was talking about; so I did.

Sitting over a cup of coffee in a noisy bar I told Terry: 'You know how things have been going between us. Well, Terry, either you are the girl for me, or you aren't. I've prayed about this; would you, too?'

I'm not sure what kind of reaction I expected, but it certainly wasn't the one I got. Terry burst into tears. 'Well, if it's all or nothing now, it's nothing!' she snapped, picking up her things and storming out of the café leaving me with two cups of coffee and a horrible feeling of failure.

Until the Venice outreach came to an end and smaller teams came together to head off for evangelism programmes all over Europe, I didn't see Terry again except for one brief exchange. I asked her to join the group I was leading on a six-week outreach to Crete. She refused coolly. She was going to Israel, she told me. Fortunately the next month-and-a-half was a busy time of leading a team, preaching and follow-up, and I didn't have much time to dwell on what had gone wrong. My team lived out on the beaches, and by the end of the programme we were all bronzed, fit and happy with the way we had seen God touching the lives of many of the young holiday-makers with whom we had come into contact.

Back in Venice the various teams came together to share stories of their successes, failures and adventures. It was thrilling to hear of some of the things that had happened, and to see how God managed to work through the enthusiasm and open-heartedness of so many students and young people.

Already my mind was taking on some of the demands of the next challenge ahead – I was to be leading our second summer of service, working on the streets of Amsterdam from our base at the campsite.

I shared details of this venture at the Venice gathering and appealed for anyone willing to join in to approach me. I couldn't resist seeking out Terry – suntanned from the outreach in Israel, looking even more lovely than ever – to ask if she wanted to come along, too. Her response was non-committal; she had to think it over.

Minutes before the bus was leaving, on our final day in Venice, Terry came to me. She seemed nervous – something I'd never noticed before.

'I've done a lot of thinking and praying, John,' she told me. 'And I've realised something ... that I really do love you, and I want to come to Amsterdam with you to see what the Lord has for us.' She would meet us in a few days.

These were the words I'd been dreaming of hearing for so long, and now they didn't seem to go in. I stared at her open-mouthed for a moment, and she smiled at my surprise. Then I smiled back as I boarded the bus. I still can't remember the trip back at all.

16

The Beach-head

We made an unusual orchestra. Dressed in overalls and shabby work clothes, we played guitars, bongos and drums as we sang our hearts out along the way. We were going to take possession of our new base in the red light district of Amsterdam, and we wanted everyone to know we were coming! We'd read again how King David had celebrated and praised as he led the Ark of the Covenant back to its rightful home, and we had decided that it was appropriate to make a thankful song and dance about our new premises too.

Following the success of our second summer out-reach, twelve months previously, we had realised that our 'commuter' programme of evangelism wasn't ideal.

The Ark wasn't far from the bustling city centre, but there wasn't room to put up a team of twenty or so without taking away from their work. The campsites were really too far out. We wanted somewhere close to the city that could be a base and a coffee bar back-up to our efforts on the streets. As I talked and prayed about this with the other leaders, we came across a rundown hotel in the centre of the red light district. It was dirty and derelict, and as a result was for sale at a ridiculously low price.

It was located in the worst part of the city's sex and drugs artery. There were sex clubs, brothels and porno cinemas on each side, and pushers and addicts on every corner. Until now YWAM's work had effectively skirted round this portion of Amsterdam; it was considered too big a challenge. But now we felt the time was right. We were spiritually strong enough to go into battle there. So, trusting God to provide the money – which he did – we had agreed to purchase the building. I was to lead in a team of volunteers that would renovate it and then use it as a base for another summer's outreach. It was a thrilling prospect.

Thirty young people had 'signed up' for the clean-up. Among them was Terry Gray. We'd had a year of ups and downs, but we were still trying to work out what our futures might be – together or apart.

Another forty or so volunteers would join us in a few weeks for the actual programme of evangelism. The Ark – the houseboats, that is – had opened their doors to us and given us room to lay our sleeping bags, side to side, while the building was made ready.

It was a great morning when we headed down into the red light district. As we neared the city quarter, famous throughout the world for its vice and drugs, we began to sing worship songs and clap our hands. Noise isn't uncommon in the district – there is music and shouting almost round the clock – but of a far different nature. So our singing began to attract curious stares from the prostitutes, pushers and pimps as we wound our way through the narrow streets.

Finally we arrived at the edge of a canal beside the Old Church, a beautiful gothic building almost six hundred years old. We stood and looked across the water to our new home; a narrow, four-storey building squeezed into one of the most notorious avenues in the whole of the neighbourhood. On either side was a satanist church, a homosexual bar, a twenty-four-hour porno cinema and drug joints. We moved round, over the small bridge and along to the front door. A great cheer went up as I turned the key in the lock and led the way into the old Budget Hotel.

It had been well named, apparently. No one could have spent any money on its upkeep in years. The building, used as a cheap hostel for students and travellers, seemed to have been deserted in an instant – like the ghost ship, the Marie Céleste – when it closed down a couple of years previously. There were plates of half-eaten food left on tables, mouldy packages in the kitchen larder, empty bottles and, more grimly, hypodermic syringes scattered all over the place. Undaunted, we burst into praise and worship. There was a huge job ahead of us, but we felt that by even just taking possession of this seedy old place we had dealt a positive blow for God in this dark area of the city. There would be battles ahead, but we had established a strong beach-head, and we sensed God's pleasure. After a final prayer of thanksgiving, we split into twos and threes to begin the huge clean-up operation.

It started in prayer. The groups headed off all over the building – a rabbit warren of a place with small, odd-shaped rooms dotted all round without any apparent sense of design or layout. In the kitchens, lounges, bathrooms and bedrooms we stopped to pray that God would sweep away any dust of evil that may have settled from the past. We claimed for God the place and the people who would live, work and visit there.

Then we rolled up our sleeves. With the job of project manager, I'd drawn up a rota of three six-hour work-shifts. It was a pattern I'd seen modelled in an Old Testament passage, and one I felt was appropriate to what we were doing. In addition, those teams not working shared a 'prayer patrol' – based in one of the small rear rooms – that ran from the moment work started until tools were finally downed late at night. We had been impressed in reading how Nehemiah had rebuilt the walls of Jerusalem to note how he had arranged for guards to watch over the workers as they laboured. We wanted every hammer blow, every stroke of the paint brush, to spring from God.

It was a filthy job. There were years of dirt and decay to tackle, but no one complained. Indeed the way in

which the teams went about their work seemed to
characterise all that we were hoping for from the new
base. They laughed and joked together as they worked,
and good humour seemed to spill from every room. It
was a profoundly marked contrast to the rest of the
area. Although there were always lots of people around
– those peddling drugs and bodies, and those buying –
there was a strong absence of warmth or personableness.
Early on we found that our new neighbours were
intrigued by our friendliness and the evident enjoyment
we had in each other's company.

One morning the work crew were stripping paint
from the front windows. They were all leaning out over
their respective window-frames, hard at work, when
someone remarked that it was just like one of those TV
game shows. There were nine windows at the front of
the building in three rows of three, each with someone
leaning out. Just like the quiz programme where the
celebrities have to answer nonsense questions. It wasn't
long before Terry had a full-blown version of the game
going in this Amsterdam sidestreet – and the squeals of
laughter gathered a small crowd. Later, as Terry recounted what had happened, she reflected sadly: 'I
couldn't work out why people looked so amazed. Then I
realised. I guess you don't get much genuine laughter
round these parts.'

We'd set ourselves a forty-day time limit – again, there
seemed to be a good precedent in the Bible – and we
just managed to finish in time before the rest of the
team joined us for the start of the actual outreach.
Their arrival stretched accommodation to the limit, so I
devised a system of three-tier bunkbeds. It meant that
people with large noses couldn't sleep on the top one,
otherwise they would be brushing the ceiling, but with a
little care and good humour we all managed to get in.

Only as we came to a special evening meeting before
our first proper outreach did we really see how important the last few dusty and yet fun-filled weeks had been.

As well as preparing the building, God had taken the time to knock us into shape. In the short space of time we had been based in the area, we had begun to sense in a new way the real spiritual oppression that hung over the neighbourhood like a big blanket. You could see it in the eyes of the people who passed by, the way they would flick away to avoid contact.

It was becoming clear to us that one of the keys to our effectiveness would be the degree to which we responded in an opposite manner. In place of furtiveness and secrecy, we wanted to display openness and honesty. And that had to begin among ourselves, in the relationships that existed in the team. We were glad to have had the time to get to know and love each other. We had come through a lot, and were looking forward to what was next.

In addition, the renovation programme had given some of the locals time to get used to our presence. There had been some uncertainty that first day we'd arrived with our songs of praise and worship. We didn't expect the suspicion to disappear overnight. In fact we were sure there would be much outright opposition in the days to come. But at least they could see that we had come to stay. Whatever followed it wasn't just going to be a hit-and-run campaign – we were the new neighbours.

At that end-of-renovation meeting, we also renewed our commitment to prayer and spiritual warfare. The importance of these two aspects of Christian service had been impressed upon me early on during my time on The Ark. In fact, I'd been told after my conversion that three of the team members had secretly been fasting and praying for me for three days before I made my commitment. From that, and my experiences in Nottingham and the early forays into Amsterdam, I knew that much of the spiritual battle took place not on the streets, but in the heavenly realms. It was there that bondages and barriers – sexual, emotional, physical and

environmental – were broken down and removed to
give an entry point for the good news about Jesus.

So prayer continued to be one of the main thrusts of
our new base. We named it The Cleft, symbolising the
source of fresh water in a desert, like that which Moses
found when he struck out with his staff. We would meet
together daily for times of worship and intercession,
asking God to move against the wickedness so evident in
the area, and to save the people who were so lost. We
would sometimes take these gatherings of praise out
onto the streets around the area, singing and praying
past the brothels and sex shops. We attracted curious
gazes, furious stares and some outright hostility. There
was even the odd barrage of water or waste food from
an upper window! We would also go out in twos,
walking round the streets praying for all the premises
and people that we passed, asking God to prepare their
hearts. We trusted that when we did go out to proclaim
the gospel, he would bring along those who were ready
to hear and respond.

Because this whole initiative was new territory for the
YWAM community in Amsterdam, we were learning
the whole time; reassessing and revising the way we
tried to reach out to people according to their particular
needs. We soon recognised that we needed to do more
than just go out, sing a few songs and then expect
people to stand and listen to someone talk about Jesus.

With its famous hurdy-gurdy machines and street
performers, Amsterdam has long been known for its
colourful city life. And with the garish attractions of the
red light district drawing crowds of tourists, we needed
something a little more visual than standard group
singing.

As I thought about this, I went back to the biography
I'd read about William Booth. I'd been so impressed
with his courage and boldness in starting the mission
work in the violent East End of London. It had struck
me, too, how clever the early Salvation Army had been

in adapting to the times. These days the brass bands are sometimes dismissed as old-fashioned and out-of-date, but they were originally formed to play the popular tunes of the day – to which were added new words that preached the gospel! After talking some of these things through with some of the other team members, we decided to take a leaf out of General Booth's book. So we held a funeral.

Some of the men in the team disappeared into The Cleft's basement and knocked up a giant-sized coffin. This was then led on a silent sorrowful procession around the red light district streets and into the Dam Square, the city's famous focal point right in front of the royal palace. By the time they got there, surprising the tourists who had gathered to feed the pigeons, the funeral party had attracted hundreds of interested men and women. The coffin was set down in the middle of the square, and as the crowd closed in, a man shot up out of the box!

It was Dave Pierce, a young American with a talent for drama and music. Face whitened and wearing dark clothes, he looked just like a corpse. But as he sprang up he began to shout and scream about how Amsterdam's sex, drugs and violence had killed him. It was startling.

All this time I would be on the other side of the square, with some other members. Discreetly mingling with the sightseers, we were the Light Team. As Dave's wails reached a peak, we would start to sing songs of praise and worship to God, and gradually make our way over to the coffin, cutting a path through the crowds. By this time the people watching wouldn't have a clue what was going on – from Dave's horrified reaction to our arrival, they wouldn't imagine we were linked in any way.

Finally as we drew near to the coffin. Dave would start shouting at me. 'Amsterdam ripped me off. There's no hope. There is no meaning to life!'

'But there is hope!' I would shout back – and we

would begin a loud debate about Jesus bringing light into people's dark lives. After a few minutes we would close abruptly and the 'mourners' and 'worshippers' would turn to talk to onlookers about what they'd seen and heard. Those who wanted to talk or hear more would be invited back to the small coffee bar we were running in the main reception area of The Cleft.

Other times we would act out the funeral at night, when we would light the way with burning torches. The procession never failed to draw hundreds of people, and we saw that it was possible to present striking images that would make people want to stop and find out more about what was going on.

We worked on other presentations, too. For what we called The Madman, there would be a regular, sober-faced, sing-for-Jesus meeting in the middle of the Dam. Only a few people would stop to listen, but we didn't expect much else – until I arrived. I'd wait until the square was fairly busy, and then make my entrance from the other side. I'd be dressed in a torn and dirty suit, with my hair dishevelled and dusty, and my arms bound to my sides with ropes. Screaming and shouting and wailing, I'd run across to the other group, stumbling and falling. I'd be shouting that Jesus couldn't help me, really attacking the 'nice little Christians' gathered there. Naturally passers-by would stop to watch the confrontation – and we'd won another audience. Many wouldn't leave the square before they'd prayed with members of the team for Christ to come into their lives.

Another small drama involved a human wall blocking off part of the square, and one of us trying to force our way through. It was a simple symbol of how we can't get into heaven by our own efforts, but it too proved effective in grabbing people's attention.

It wasn't all easy, though. We accepted that you couldn't really preach the gospel without risking people's wrath, or offending the unseen spiritual enemy.

I'm on top of a small table, and there's a good crowd standing back to listen. I scan the faces as I talk, and I can see the familiar reactions; amusement, scorn, intrigue, awkwardness, interest, suspicion, mocking. It never ceases to amaze me that people will stop and watch someone eating fire or swallowing razor blades in the open air without thinking anything of it, but get up and start talking about God and they suddenly become very edgy.

Open-air preaching is a little like performing from a stage. You've got to work your audience well, and I'm constantly darting my eyes over those listening as I talk to them in short bursts. I'm telling them about how my life was turned upside down by a seeming 'chance' encounter just a few hundred yards away and then I pick up some sense of disturbance out of the corner of my eye. Turning, but not breaking my delivery, I spot three young men stepping through the crowd and into the kind of 'no-man's land' of open space that's always left between a street preacher and his audience. It's as though people don't want to come too close in case you reach out and try to snatch them into God's hands. When they break that invisible barrier, I know it means trouble.

A quick prayer as I continue to talk without apparent concern. Complete outward assurance and confidence is one of the absolute keys of open-air preaching, we've learned. Show any sense of not being in control and you've lost your territory and the attention you can command. 'Help me handle this one, please Lord,' I ask behind my spoken words.

The three lads have marched up to the table, and they're trying to drag me off. 'Shut up, or we'll make you!' one snarls. I'm told later that they were heaving and pulling for all they were worth, but all I feel is fluttery touches like birds' wings, so I carry on talking and ignore them. 'What shall I do now, God?' I ask as I sense the concern in the faces of some of the listeners.

Responding to that quiet-but-clear voice inside which I've learned to trust, I squat down until I'm face to face with the lead protagonist. He's thick-necked, crop-haired and clearly looking for a fight.

I lean forward and say to him, as quietly and calmly as I can manage: 'In the name of Jesus I rebuke and bind you violent spirits, and I command you to leave this square. Now!' I straighten up to carry on preaching, heart racing but unafraid deep down.

The light of fight switches off in the faces of the other two immediately – it's a transformation I've often seen in moments of spiritual confrontation. The other hesitates for a moment before turning to the crowd with a sneer. 'D'you know what this bloke's just said to me? He's just told me to go away – in Jesus' name!' The last is uttered with a roar of harsh laughter but, nevertheless, he shrugs his shoulders and leads his two friends off.

Thanking God for helping me through, I finish my story of conversion and reflect again on the commitment I've made. My job is to preach the gospel on the streets, like this, and I can't afford to let anything, or anyone, intimidate me.

We learned that the fear of man was a major stumbling block to effectiveness in streetwork. If someone in the team was worried or anxious about what people might say or do in response, then their efforts were shackled. Usually after a couple of days' experience and plenty of prayer, they found themselves able to let go of all their concerns and trust God for their safety and sense of value.

There were rare moments of threatened physical violence – these were usually resolved by silent spiritual warfare and claiming Jesus' authority over the disruptive spirits trying to stop what we were doing. More common was the emotional aggression we'd face from people offended by the idea that a God of love should have to die for them because of their failure to live according to his standards. Usually this could be channelled into positive times of talking and discussion, particularly when we broke up into ones and twos to mingle with the crowds. On other occasions, though, we'd be left with an earful of abuse.

Many days there would be no apparent results from our efforts, no interest. At these times it was easy to feel discouraged and to question the value of the time and effort we were putting in, but as we prayed together and came to God asking him about it we were renewed again in our determination to keep going and trust God for the rest.

One key spiritual victory involved the cults that flourished in the city. The whirlpool of drugs and liberal philosophies in the city attracted every kind of fringe religion – and they all wanted their opportunity to 'recruit'.

From the start of our streetwork I felt that the Dam Square was crucial. The largest public open space in the city, under the façade of the royal palace, it hosts fairs and performing troupes, and always has a crowd of sightseers. In addition, I sensed that it symbolised 'ownership' of the city and that God wanted it.

We staged regular prayer walks, agreeing together for the Lord's name to be honoured over all others on the Dam. We found that other groups using the area – notably Hare Krishna and Bhagwan devotees – were beginning to stay away. They'd walk up to the edge of the Dam from one of the adjoining streets, stop, then skirt round the edge as though prevented from coming any closer by an invisible force field.

Even with all the excitement of the new base and the new ministry, my thoughts were never far from Terry. We'd managed to find time to be together during those hectic days of renovation and preparation, until I was confident enough about asking her to marry me.

One night at The Ark I took Terry into what had been the captain's quarters. I'd lit a row of candles to create just the right atmosphere for what I hoped was the perfect moment. I took hold of her hand and told her: 'Terry, I love you. I want you to be my wife. Will you marry me?'

She looked wonderful in the soft candlelight. 'I need some time to think,' she responded.

I was taken aback. 'But ... why ... what?'

'I just need time. I have to ask my father,' she explained.

'But that could take ages!' I was frustrated at her idea. It could take a long time for her to go to America and talk it over with her parents. Terry sensed how my thoughts were going.

'No, John. I mean my heavenly Father!' she smiled.

I was still anxious to know, but I reckoned that at least this wouldn't take so long. So I smiled and agreed.

And a couple of nights later we were crossing the Ij on a ferry – just up from The Ark – when Terry told me: 'John, I'm ready to answer you now. Ask me again.' The stars were twinkling, the water rushed past below us as we stood looking over the side, her hair streaming in the wind. Her answer was: 'Yes.' We headed back to The Cleft that night, hand in hand, with a wedding to plan.

17

Firm Foundations

It was a seedy threshold, but we hardly noticed. I swept Terry up into my arms, and carried her into our new home – being careful not to bump her limbs on the narrow walls. It was a tight squeeze. Home was a single small room tucked away at the rear of The Cleft. It wasn't the sort of quiet, clean place you would normally expect to find newlyweds, but we didn't mind. We were happy, we were together – and we knew that God was with us in our marriage.

Ten days earlier we had exchanged vows and rings in the gardens of Heidebeek. A beautifully crisp, clear autumn day, with the fallen leaves from the trees layering the grass in what looked like a carpet of woven gold and amber. The fairytale picture had been completed when the music group struck up the bridal march, and I turned to see Terry as she walked towards me. All my nervousness at having to remember my 'lines' evaporated as I looked at her in wonder. Walking on the arm of her father, wrapped in a gorgeous white dress, she looked like a dream. I stole a look at my best man, Peter Gruschka, and thought again of all that had happened over the previous few years. As Terry looked at me and smiled, I silently thanked God for this wonderful new life he had given me – and this lovely wife: beautiful, fun and with a heart that longed to see others find Jesus.

It was terrific to share this moment with all those who mattered to me. Mum was in the front row, dressed in

her best new frock and beaming from ear to ear like the
Queen Mother. Joan and Sean were there, as well as
Trish and Jamie – a love story from the early days of the
Nottingham fellowship – and their baby son. Peter
Gruschka was the best man, Paul Miller and Paul Filler
were two of the stewards, and standing in front of us to
conduct the service was dear Floyd, looking down with a
twinkle in his eye and a smile that threatened to split his
cheeks.

Friends of Terry's performed a lovely dance to a song
of worship and, after more songs of praise, we were
eventually pronounced man and wife. We walked hand-
in-hand down the grassy aisle, and as soon as we reached
the main building we took off, running out of sight.

Safely hidden around the corner, we stood to get our
breath back, looked into each other's eyes and laughed
aloud with sheer delight.

During the reception, friends from home and The
Ark and students at the current Discipleship Training
School kept coming up to me to slip their hands into my
jacket pocket. I later found wads of notes – all gifts for
our honeymoon. Through Floyd, a wealthy Christian
businessman had made available his countryside retreat.
It was a secluded holiday cottage up in the hills near the
Baltic Sea, not far from the Danish border. And it was
all ours!

We were thrilled by this surprise provision, and after
our wedding night in a small hotel, we drove by borrowed car to our holiday destination … and had an
early lesson in the way our married life would go. It was
getting late in the day and we were just outside Bremen,
hammering along the autobahn, when the Audi started
to judder and slow. 'Quick, pull over!' I shouted to
Terry, who was having a spell at driving, and she managed
to guide us to the side of the road. An exit was just ahead,
and as the car continued to lose power we managed to
coast up to the junction roundabout, cross it and finally
come to a halt at the side of a small link road.

It was pitch dark by this time, and we were in a fairly remote spot. There was little passing traffic and no sign of help. I tried everything I knew about fixing tired engines, but nothing seemed to work. 'Come on, Terry, let's pray. God has got us this far. He won't let us down now, I know.' We bowed our heads together and asked for help.

We had barely opened our eyes again when a small car appeared out of nowhere and pulled onto the side of the road in front of us. Terry and I looked at each other in surprise – but there was more to follow. The driver got out and walked back towards us; a little man with a round, kindly face and sparkly eyes. I moved to get out to join him, but he just smiled and motioned to me to sit tight. Then he went back to his car, pulled a tow rope out of the boot and connected it to our front bracket. With a smile, the next thing we knew he was back in his driving seat, and we were being pulled off down the road.

With half an eye on the road ahead, I tried to catch another glimpse of the couple in the car in front. The lady in the passenger seat turned and her face was wreathed in a kindly, encouraging smile. She nodded her head gently as if to say 'It's OK' and our follow-the-leader journey continued. After a few minutes we found ourselves rolling into a garage with a connecting hotel. We coasted to a halt on the forecourt and one of the attendants came over to my window.

Distracted for a moment, I didn't turn back until Terry called: 'John, they're going!' Sure enough the couple with the gentle faces had packed the tow rope away and were driving off, with a final backward smile and wave. They hadn't spoken a single word throughout the entire 'rescue', nor waited for us to be able to express our gratitude.

As they pulled away, we turned to each other and said simultaneously: 'Do you think that they...?' and we laughed aloud at the idea that hit us both.

There was no mechanic on duty, so we spent the night at the adjacent hotel. The next morning, after half an hour or so of scratching his head under our bonnet, the mechanic declared that there was nothing wrong – which a flick of the ignition switch proved. It started first time. Even more perplexing!

As we drove on once more, we reminded each other of the previous night's curious happenings, and the strange way we had come to find such a romantic stopover.

This sense of God's intimate concern and care for us was to prove a rock in the months that followed. For things didn't work out as we had anticipated. The plan had been for us to return to Terry's South Carolina hometown. I'd secured a place at a respected Bible College – I felt as though it was important to do some more serious studying before moving on further in Christian service – and we wanted some time in which Terry's parents, friends and home church could come to know me more, and I them. In addition, we believed that it was vital for our new relationship to be given some room in which to grow and blossom, away from the harshness and busyness of work in inner-city Amsterdam.

But the temporary stay we had planned at The Cleft for a week – between the end of our honeymoon and our flight out to the States – turned into six months. And it heralded the start of another new initiative in evangelism.

My criminal record was the problem. Those past convictions created all sorts of concerns for the authorities whose job it was to give me the relevant paperwork allowing me to reside in America. Extra forms and declarations had to be completed and made, and we were advised that it could be several weeks, if not months, before it was all sorted out. It was a frustration we hadn't expected, but we decided to make the most of our time by earning some extra money.

The YWAM community agreed to let us stay on at
The Cleft, and I picked up my bricklaying toolbag once
more and went back onto the sites. I found work on a
huge civic flats complex being constructed on the out-
skirts of the city. The work schedule meant that I had to
be up at 5:30 am to be on site by 7 am. So I found myself
going to bed mid-evening to ensure I got enough sleep –
just when Terry's 'nightbird' character was coming to
life. Accentuated by the cramped quarters, those early
weeks created some tensions as we learned to love our
way round the practical difficulties that faced our new
life together.

As the weeks stretched into months, the waiting
became much harder for Terry. Working on the sites,
all my energies were absorbed in earning money. So I
didn't have much left over for worrying about The Cleft
and its work. In fact it was good to have a break from all
the responsibilities of leading such a project. I hoped
that if and when I returned to such a role, it would be
with a freshness and new vigour. But for Terry it was
different. She wasn't working, and being in and around
the building all day, she was more keenly aware of the
struggles that were going on in order for the base we
had opened up some months before to find its feet with
a permanent role. Some of those who had helped in the
renovation and summer evangelism had stayed on as
full-time team members, but the future direction of The
Cleft was still unclear.

The seeds of something new were sown as Terry
talked with me in the evenings. She told me how she and
other girls living at The Cleft were concerned about the
prostitutes who worked in the area right round the
building. The working girls hire windowed rooms in the
houses up and down the canal streets where – backlit by
a red glow – they sit on view semi-nude, advertising
their 'wares' to the passing crowds. When someone
wants business, they just step inside and close the
curtains.

Several thousand prostitutes work this way in Amsterdam's red light district, and the brazen way they operate attracts guided tours of holiday-makers filing past the city's infamous liberal sex shops and brothels.

'These people are our neighbours, you know, John,' Terry said one night. 'I just don't feel that I can walk past them like I do every day – going to the shops, or the park – and not try to reach out to them . . . without losing my integrity as a Christian. I've got to try. But what can I do?'

I was excited to see her being moved in this way, and we prayed together to ask God to show the next step. A few nights later Terry told me that she and another Cleft girl with whom she regularly prayed – Mientje Brouwer, a part-time nurse – had agreed they should set a date on which they would go out and try to make contact with one of the prostitutes in the neighbourhood.

It was to be the following Tuesday.

It's been another long and tiring day, but I almost run up the steep stairs at The Cleft. My thoughts have returned to Terry and Mientje often during the day, and now I'll get to hear how it went. Up in our room Terry's waiting, looking elated. I make us both a hot drink and sit down facing her to hear the story. Her excitement bubbles over as she recounts their first efforts at reaching out to the prostitutes.

As the clock ticked towards the late-morning starting time they had set themselves, Terry and Mientje met together again for prayer. They asked God to lead them to just the right person. 'And,' Terry says, 'we didn't know what to do, so we asked the Lord to show us. We felt him say that we were to buy some flowers and just walk right on in and shut the door.' She smiles with glee. 'So we did!'

I can tell from her bubbly mood that the story gets better, so I urge her to go on. 'Well, what happened next?'

'We went out and walked round the nearest streets. And d'you know, all the windows were empty. We couldn't believe it! It isn't so busy at that time of the day, of course, but there wasn't a single girl to be seen. We even wondered for a moment if we'd got it wrong. But we decided to keep looking, and finally we found just one window with a girl there – and we decided that this must be the one the Lord was leading us to,' Terry relates.

'We were really nervous, so we just walked in quickly and shut the door behind us hard. Poor girl. I'm sure she didn't know what to think! Anyway, I just said, "Hi, we've moved into the area. We just came to introduce ourselves and chat for a while. Here are some flowers." And we got talking, just like that. We were able to tell her that we are Christians, and what we are all doing here at The Cleft. She was really listening, you know – not anxious to get rid of us or anything. In fact she let us pray for her just before we finally left. Her eyes were watery as she told us that she didn't really want to be here in the red light district, but that she needed the money and she couldn't think of any other way of getting it.'

Terry's elation at their contact is dimmed as she recalls the girl's sad story, and her eyes fill with tears.

'On the way back we prayed that she'd get away from this place and find some other work. Oh John, do you think that God can really do something in the lives of people like that?'

'Sure,' I answer. 'It won't be easy, of course. But the Holy Spirit can touch the hardest of hearts. He did mine, remember?'

We sit down together in our poky little bedroom and pray for the girls in all the scores of other rooms within close proximity of The Cleft, and ask God to help Terry and the others in their efforts at bridge-building.

Most days after that Terry and Mientje, followed by the other staff women, would either go out on prayer walks for the girls they passed in the windows, or make contact with them. They would take a gift of flowers – a Dutch custom – or pack a thermos of coffee into a basket together with some biscuits, and go into the rooms to offer refreshments. Sometimes they met sharp words and stony faces. Other times they found open ears and bruised hearts.

And we discovered in a new way the reality of the unseen battle that was being fought over the red light area. Some evenings I'd return home after a hard day, and almost as soon as I reached for the door handle of our room, I would know that Terry had been out visiting the prostitutes. I could sense a presence of evil, wickedness, in the room – just as though she'd stepped in something that didn't smell too sweet and had brought it back on her heel. We learned to pray hard and bind the enemy from our home and our lives. Terry began to pray for protection before every visit, and then for a special cleansing of the Holy Spirit as she left, so that she wouldn't be 'contaminated' by coming into contact with people so clearly bound by the enemy.

On occasions, though, it would be a struggle. One particular woman she visited was unyielding and in-hospitable – yet Terry felt it right to keep going back from time to time, trying to show love and care. 'Every time I go in, it is like walking into a mental fog,' she told me. 'Sometimes I really have to struggle to get the next word out of my mouth. There is a terrible feeling of tightness round my head, just like someone is screwing on a metal band. And I find it hard to get my breath, as though there is a great weight bearing down on me. It's scary at times.'

The more she and the other girls at The Cleft worked with the prostitutes, the better we understood their plight. And it made us desperately sad. We could see how poverty, greed, anger and rejection were often woven into the lives of these women. There were young girls still with childish faces and teenage bodies and older women, some even grandmothers. Some were there because they were illegal immigrants in Holland and couldn't get a regular job. Others had been abused at home or unwanted and had run away. They needed to support themselves. Some were there to support their own or their partner's drug or alcohol habits. Others needed money to help pay for their children's clothes and meals because they couldn't manage as single parents. One respectable young wife was there because she and her husband wanted to open a tennis training centre and needed the capital!

Six months had almost rolled round by the time we were finally given clearance to leave for the States. But we were no longer too frustrated. Looking back we could see the reason for the delay. Terry had been instrumental in beginning a whole new initiative in YWAM's evangelism in the city, and as we left, there were plans to consolidate it with extra workers and prayer support. We were pleased and excited, and felt that in some small way the work had already been 'approved' by God. The young woman Terry and Mientje had visited on that first morning had not been seen in the district since.

From the crowded backstreets of Amsterdam's maze of brothels, porno cinemas and sex shops, suburbia USA was a shock. But we quickly came to love the airiness, lightness and freedom – physically and spiritually – that there was to enjoy.

Terry and I found ourselves a second-floor apartment not far from her parents' spacious home. It was well appointed, with fitted carpets and all utilities, and we revelled in the space after the squeeze of The Cleft. The apartment building had a pool right outside our door where Terry would swim most mornings before breakfast and going to work. It was a time of real refreshment and enjoyment. It was good, too, to grow closer to Terry's parents. They had been very nice to me the only time I'd seen them before the wedding, during a brief visit to the States. But it had understandably been a little strained. I'd been nervous at what they would think of me, and overwhelmed by their large home and standard of living. The large detached house in its own spacious grounds was a far cry from my childhood slums.

But during our time in America we grew to know and love each other. As I learned more about them, I came deeply to respect their love and care for their family, and the faithful way they supported their friends and their local church. If they didn't quite understand the way we wanted to live, serving God in a foreign country with no apparent concern for the practicalities of life and little income, then they didn't show it.

Almost before we knew it, January had rolled round and it was time for us to return to Amsterdam. We had kept in touch with Floyd and the others, and heard how they had acquired another large building in the city. A former grand hotel and the one-time Salvation Army headquarters that had been over-run by squatters for years had finally been vacated, and YWAM had taken it on. Standing on the edge of the red light district, it was only a few snaky streets away from The Cleft, and strategically placed for the city centre.

In addition, the YWAM leaders were looking for us to help lead a DTS and some new evangelism work in the city when we got back. Rested, happy, established, we flew back to Europe keen for a new challenge.

One small problem was that we didn't have much support. All YWAM workers joined 'in faith'. There were no wages, and they looked for friends and home churches to back them in meeting their needs as they served in missions. Because of the way our paths had led, Terry and I didn't have many folk who knew what we were involved in, so we had only a few pounds a week to live on.

It clearly wasn't enough to find somewhere to rent, particularly in water-ringed Amsterdam, where building development is restricted and rooms are at a premium.

But Floyd came to our rescue. 'We're still renovating the Samaritan's Inn, but there's a spare room there, if you are interested at all,' he offered.

He took us round. And at first I thought he'd shown us the broom cupboard by mistake! There wasn't enough room to swing a cat, if it had a long tail. Neither was there a washbasin, and the toilets were on the next floor. With renovation work going on all round, it was like living in the middle of a building site. But it was to be our home for two years.

After some initial tears from Terry and frustrated attempts to find somewhere else, we knuckled down to making the most of what we had, and being thankful for it. I constructed a bed on stilts, so that we had to climb up close to the ceiling to go to sleep, but it meant that there was space underneath for living during the day. We could just about squeeze two chairs in when we had guests, and with some pretty pictures on the walls we did our best to make it home.

As we asked God to help us to be happy with our lot, he answered our prayers. We grew to love our little corner, and if ever we started to murmur again inside we only had to look to what was happening outside – in the streets around – to know that it was no accident that we were there.

For God was at work, and we were excited to be part of the action.

18

Still Burning

We were running a full programme of outreaches on Amsterdam's streets. Music, drama and dance were all being employed to draw a crowd with whom we could share the gospel. It was tiring, thrilling, frustrating, rewarding ... but it still wasn't enough. I felt we needed yet another way of trying to grab people's attention, one that managed to capture their curiosity while at the same time making an unequivocal statement of what we were about.

So we built a large cross. A group of guys went down to the basement again, as they had when the coffin first appeared, and took apart a packing case. With some saw cuts and bolts they constructed a huge wooden cross, standing over eleven feet tall and weighing forty pounds. Just standing in front of it as we heaved it up straight made me realise in a new way what Jesus had done when he died for our sins at Calvary. It made my heart race in thankfulness and gratitude; and I sensed that it would provoke similarly strong feelings out on the streets.

Some were clearly offended by the visual statement. They would stop briefly to shout and curse at us before stamping off. Others stayed to hear what we had to say as we preached from beneath the apex. But the full impact of the cross was only brought home to us when we were visited by someone who knew its power from years of personal experience.

Arthur Blessitt had started walking round the world with his cross twenty years before, and many thousands of miles later he was still going. By the time he arrived in Amsterdam he had experienced extraordinary things in scores of countries – and repeatedly seen the incredible way in which God uses the very symbol of his love to touch people's lives and to transform them. Arthur was used to attracting huge crowds out of which hundreds would kneel on the streets to commit their lives to Christ there and then, weeping before friends and family without a thought for how others would view them.

As he joined our street teams for a couple of weeks, we felt a clear confirmation for our cross plans. We built five others, and had teams carrying them all over the city for meetings and outreaches. In fact, they became such a common sight that a young German girl visiting the city stopped and observed to one of the team members that Amsterdam must be a very Christian city, because everywhere she went there were people carrying crosses. She wouldn't have needed to stay in the city much longer, or ventured much further, to have discovered things to be otherwise!

One morning we had set the cross up on the open ground in front of the Central Station, and I was preaching in front of the cross. As I spoke, an angry-looking man stepped out of the crowd and pulled the microphone from my hand. I let him take it, and he threw it to the ground, cursing and abusing me. I stepped back a pace or two to give him a wide berth, but just carried on talking, raising my voice to make sure that those at the back could still hear. Past experience told me to keep an eye on the intruder, so I kept him in the corner of my sight. Suddenly he lunged forward, fist bunched to strike me in the face. I braced myself for the blow – which never came. Just before his punch landed, I saw the man pitch through the air, landing on the ground with a crash. He lay there unmoving. The meeting was brought to an abrupt halt as we called an ambulance to the scene to take the injured man away to hospital, and I discovered what had happened.

The shouting man had been felled by a huge ox of a man who was standing nearby. The attacker wasn't a Christian, but he had spent some time talking with Arthur Blessitt in a city park a couple of days earlier, and the encounter had so impressed him that he didn't want any of Arthur's friends to have any trouble!

Arthur's brief visit confirmed for me that the streets were my 'pulpit', and that was the way it would stay. Secretly, I'd sometimes thought in the past that my days leading that kind of outreach were limited; that in some way they were an apprenticeship for when I'd be preaching at big missions and rallies. In Arthur I saw a man totally committed to doing what God wanted him to, and ignoring the pressures for anything else. He was a man walking close to Jesus who knew that success could not be counted in worldly terms, and as a result the Holy Spirit was able to work miracles through his unassuming, everyday life. And I realised that the open air, the pavements, the shopping malls were what I knew, and where I was most comfortable.

By now our work in Amsterdam was beginning to attract interest and attention from around the world – other YWAM groups, local churches, Bible Colleges and mission organisations. During the summer we ran large, short-term projects which drew in young people from all over the world. Many of them went back to their home churches enthusiastic about all they had experienced, and we began to get enquiries about taking what we were doing to new places. And so a new initiative was born: GO Teams, standing for Global Outreach.

The idea was to bring together a team of men and women interested in short-term mission work, give them some basic discipleship training and grounding in all we had learned about street evangelism, and then to earth all that in several weeks of 'on the job' training. This would involve us travelling for up to four months – across Europe, India, or parts of northern Africa – and taking part in evangelism alongside local churches in cities, towns and even remote villages along the way. By being fairly small, mobile and independent, we could aim to take the gospel to even the out-of-the-way places. The people there had as much need to hear about Jesus as anywhere else.

As we planned, it became clear that some of the things we did in Amsterdam were peculiar to that city. We couldn't hope to repeat the funeral procession or the cross march in other parts of Europe and have the same results. So we needed another new way of drawing people together. Talented Dave Pierce came up with the solution once more.

He pointed us to *Toymaker and Son*, a musical parable about creation, the fall of man and salvation through Jesus. Mixing drama and dance, the fifty-minute production had little narration and no dialogue, although its message soon became clear. At the end there would be a clear opportunity to step forward and talk some more about what people had just witnessed.

Working on *Toymaker*, we devised a series of costumes that could clearly depict the different characters and yet at the same time easily 'travel' to different parts and be recognisable. And so it was that I found myself dressed up like an overgrown Pinocchio – complete with knicker-bockers and white knee-socks – for my part as The Toymaker.

Packing all our kit, clothing and possessions into an old Swedish city bus, our small team of eighteen set off for a four-month cross-Europe trek. We would arrive in a village or town about mid-day, and through local pastors who would pre-arrange permits begin to pre-pare for an outreach, having joined with local Christians in prayer. In the early evening we would begin to set out the simple 'staging' and music system in the town square or largest plot of open land available. This would quickly draw a crowd, and by the time we were ready to perform – usually about nine or ten o'clock – word of mouth would have brought a large crowd to see the visiting players. The piece required a small baby, and by this time we were able to replace the plastic doll used in the early *Toymaker* days with our own son, Sandy, who was fourteen months old.

Once the performing and preaching were over, there would often be conversations that carried on until well after midnight. Many times, too, these one-to-one talks would be followed with prayers in which people asked Jesus into their lives. The local Christians would translate for us, and would invite them to their churches the following week. With the twin demands of leading the team and caring for a toddler in primitive travelling conditions, Terry and I found it hard work – but the nightly rewards kept us going. For several summers we trailed *Toymaker* across Spain, Italy, Portugal, Greece and England.

It was strange to be back in Nottingham again, especially with my Toymaker costume on. At the end of the performance I was able to stand up, as I had done so many times before, and point out the places from my past: the wine lodge, the jeweller's shop that I had robbed, the alleys in which I'd fought and thieved.

We were packing everything into the bus when someone tapped me on the shoulder. 'John, it *is* you, isn't it? Johnny Goodfellow?'

I turned round and saw a friend from the old days. Short and stocky, Terry had been another hard man. A boxer of some renown, he'd not been shy of using his skills outside the ring when the need arose. I was surprised to find him watching *Toymaker*. We chatted casually for a few minutes, but I sensed we were skating round the issue. Finally he managed to find the words. 'I came down because I saw you on the telly the other night. D'you remember?'

I did. A reporter for the local TV station had come down to investigate what we were doing in the town centre during our week's stay. They had been interested to learn that I was an 'old boy' of the town, and they had run a short film report about *Toymaker*, including a brief interview with me as the 'reformed' villain.

'Well, I was dead surprised to see you like that, and to hear what you were saying. So I decided to come down to see for myself what it was all about. I want to know more, John. You really have changed, you know.'

There wasn't time for more right there and then, so I invited him to come over to visit us in Amsterdam a few weeks later. He came, bringing his teenage son with him, telling a story of a lot of pain – including a broken marriage – and thoughts of suicide. When Terry and James flew back to the Midlands the next week, they had both given their lives to Jesus.

Another person touched by *Toymaker* during our English visit was a reporter for one of the local papers. He managed to make contact with me, and we agreed to meet for an interview at a motorway service station. For the first twenty minutes or so his questions were for his article. But for the next ninety minutes they were his own search. The coffees we nursed went cold as he asked me more and more about God.

This time the outcome wasn't as encouraging. When we parted he told me: 'I believe it's all true, you know – everything that you've said about Jesus dying for our sins and all that. I believe it. It's just that ... I can't give what it demands of you. I like women, you see, and I'm just not prepared to make that kind of sacrifice. I don't want to become a monk.' He'd got his story, but he'd not been able to cope with the facts.

In the early days, his rejection would have troubled me. But over the years I had met every kind of response to the gospel. As well as conviction and tears of joy and laughter, there had been venom, scorn, ridicule, uninterest, unbelief and suspicion. I had learned not to worry, but to trust God to work in the lives of those we met, at his pace. Maybe our contact would be the first of several that would eventually lead to Christ. Or perhaps they had already made their choice. It wasn't for me to try to work it all out – just to keep going, talking and praying, trusting that God would prepare the people with whom we would come into contact, and to leave the rest to him.

There were many times when the last thing I wanted to do was to go out onto the streets and preach. I felt tired or discouraged, or maybe the cutting remark overheard from the last outreach was still in my mind; but at these times we learned just to keep going. The closeness we've had in our teams has been a real bonus. And the faith of those who invited us to help them reach their city has helped us through the tough days.

And when the time wasn't right for street work, there were always other possibilities. . . .

Even the rain hasn't driven the hordes of tourists from the streets. They are still milling round the window girls, the sex shops and the pushers, who casually and openly badger you to buy – 'Cocaine, hash . . . I've got the best . . . come on, man' – like they are selling souvenir rosettes outside a football ground. So it's good to step off the streets for a while – into the bars.

This is one of my favourites. A step down and we're in a poky, musty little backstreet place that's about as clean and well decorated as a coal cellar. Its ceiling is tiled with fading beer mats, and there are small lights in each of the drinking booths around the wall. When you look closely at the cracked dirty tables, you're glad that the lighting is dim. It's better not to see too much.

But this place is always busy. The guys come in for a beer and a laugh as they ogle their way round the red light district. And right in the middle of the floor, taking up most of the room, is the pool table. It's such a tight squeeze that when you're taking a shot from the sides you have to hold the cue up in the air at about a forty-five degree angle, otherwise the end gets jammed against the wall. It makes for a more interesting game, though – and as a regular, I'm used to it.

I'd been looking for another way of getting alongside people when it struck me how popular pool is. So I spent some months practising in the lunch-hour, and now I come out two or three evenings a week, drifting round the bars to shoot a few games and see if there is any opportunity for conversation.

The winner stays on the table, taking on the next challenger, so it's useful to know a few shots. And if you can shoot a good game, the other players tend to give you some respect, so it opens up more doors. There's no point beating around the bush, so as we're playing I'll get straight to the point. I ask them where they are from and what they're doing. When they respond and ask me the same, I tell them: 'I'm an evangelist.'

Sometimes they shut up, sometimes they change the subject. But on occasions they want to know more, so we'll talk. It's amazing to think about some of the conversations I've had with guys in one of the booths around this bar, deep in the city's brothel quarter.

One time in particular I remember pulling out all the stops to beat two youngsters. They were from a party of six Englishmen visiting the city for 'a dirty weekend'. As we got talking, I found out that they were all local pool champions for their area. And I beat them all! God must have been helping me play above par for a reason. They invited me over to their table, where they had a crate of beers stacked, and I was able to tell them my testimony during the next hour. There were two of them, especially, that night who wanted to hear more about Jesus.

Tonight it's quiet. I nod at the barman. He recognises me as a regular and presents me with a Coke. Sipping, I slip my guilder over the edge of the table to claim the next game, settle back into a seat in the corner and look around. As I do I pray again: 'Well, Father, if there's someone here tonight that you want me to talk to, then I trust you to bring them to me.'

It's my turn at the table. He breaks, but fails to put

anything away. I slice a stripe into the centre pocket, lining the cue ball up for a second stripe down in the far corner. We're off.

As we make polite chit-chat between shots, I learn he's from Germany. A student, touring the Continent during his vacation, and staying at The Shelter while he's in the city. It makes me smile to myself.

Casually we get there. 'What about you? What do you do for a living?'

'Me? I'm an evangelist.'

'What do you mean?'

'I'm a Christian, and I work with a group of people in the city here. We try to help people by telling them about Jesus. Have you ever thought about God much?'

This could turn out to be a late night. But thankfully the bar stays open almost until the last customer leaves, or falls asleep.

Over the past few years I've preached on the streets hundreds of times. Usually I've shared God's love in the only way I really know how; telling folk about what happened to me when I found myself at the end of my own efforts, and he stepped in. I've told essentially the same story so many times that, in one way, I could almost recite it in my sleep.

But in another way, it's fresh every time. Recalling the days and nights of lostness, loneliness and emptiness when I desperately tried to fill the hollowness up with drugs, or drink, or sex, or occult experiences. And as I retrace my steps, my heart fills with joy at knowing how God hasn't just changed my life. He's literally saved it.

For I'm pretty sure that if that intervention hadn't come near Amsterdam's Central Station, then I'd have been dead by now. My anger, violence and desperation were spinning more and more out of control, and it wouldn't have been long before they would have pitched me into something too far, too wild, too much.

All these thoughts and feelings spill around inside as I

talk to the crowds, and then individually, one-to-one. It's a simple love for Jesus and all that he has done for me, and it's thrilling to be part of something that changes someone's life for all eternity. Just before I start to preach, I remind myself that there are people listening who are going to respond – even there and then – and commit their lives to Christ. And to think they had no idea when they left home that morning!

Just like the man in Rome, who just happened to meet our GO team. He had gone out for an ice cream with his daughter when he was attracted by the noise and crowd. *Toymaker* was in town. Drawn to the drama, he paused to watch for a few moments and found himself gripped. He told us later that he simply couldn't pull himself away.

After the preaching, he and his daughter were among the first to step forward and ask to be prayed with to accept Jesus as their Saviour. The very next evening he returned to the square with his wife and other daughter, and wept with tears of joy as they too chose to become Christians.

Then there was Danny. He was planning a murder when he and his wife strolled past a street team in Amsterdam's pretty Vondel Park. A well-known criminal in the city, he'd been ripped off by an associate, and he was scheming to make the man pay with his life. But he pricked up his ears as he heard me preaching about how I had been a thief and a criminal. They both stopped to listen to what I had to say. When approached by one of the team afterwards, first his wife and then he bowed their heads and prayed for forgiveness for their sins.

Libby wasn't looking for more than a good time when we bumped into her and a friend near the Dam Square one day. They had paused to stare at an open air rally being conducted by another group of Christians. Together with a friend I managed to get chatting to them, and later that night at The Ark she said a simple prayer of commitment. The result was dramatic. When she arrived for work on Monday morning, Libby was

surrounded by her friends, all clamouring to know:
'What happened to you over the weekend? You look
incredible.' Her face continued to glow as she told them:
'I met Jesus.'

Many more similar stories come to mind: people physically healed by the Lord; people set free from terrible
bondages of evil; those released from deep emotional
hurts from their past. And all through knowing Jesus.

But I don't want to end this book by telling you
another story. Instead I want to close by challenging you
to take the opportunity of featuring in your own.

If you have read this far and you're not a Christian,
then you need to decide whether you think what I've
recounted is fact or fantasy. If you accept that it's true,
then I believe you will need to respond by giving your
life to Christ. There's a brief prayer to help you in the
afterword on the following pages. Please turn to it right
now.

If you are a Christian, then I would hope you've
finished this book having been encouraged in one of two
areas, or maybe both.

First to believe that God can use you to reach the rest
of your family if they don't know him. Even if there are
big barriers, he can repair relationships so that you are
able to share the good news of the gospel, through
words and actions. It may take time and some tears, but
I'm convinced that after we have been restored to our
heavenly Father, he wants to see us restored to our
earthly fathers ... and mothers, sisters, brothers, and
children.

And I want you to be stirred for evangelism: to see
that every day there are countless people who are lost
and hurt, who through a 'chance' encounter – because
someone's left a purse behind, or they are buying an ice
cream – get to hear the fantastic message of salvation.

All they need is for someone along the way to be
available to tell them. That's the key: availability. Not
personality or ability. Not everyone is called to street

evangelism and open air preaching – although we've found through our short-term mission initiatives that once many try it they wonder why they've waited so long to get involved!

It is simply a question of responding to Jesus' commission in Matthew 28, when he says: 'All authority in heaven and on earth has been given to me. Therefore go and make disciples of all nations.'

Where you have to 'go' may be a foreign city, thousands of miles from home; or your local shopping precinct on a Saturday, with a drama team and singing group; or the mothers-and-toddlers group, where people are looking for friendship; or your school or office, where the name of Jesus is only heard as a swear word.

But don't leave it for someone else to do.

One recent summer I felt the Lord calling me to walk with a cross in Africa. I trained for several weeks by humping a backpack full of bricks round the Amsterdam streets. Then I packed a few spare clothes and flew out to Zambia. For a fortnight I carried a large cross down into the centre of the city each day, prayed and preached. My team comprised just five local people, including a housewife and a teenage girl. Around five hundred people gave their lives to Christ while I was there; it was great to be around as people responded to the gospel so openly.

I expect that there will be other trips like that in the future. I hope so! New initiatives in evangelism continue to develop in Amsterdam where I serve on the YWAM council, and the GO teams are still operating year by year. Other young evangelists and leaders are emerging. It's exciting to see the ways in which God is using and leading them.

After our sons Sandy and Jason grow up, Terry and I do have a little idea tucked away at the back of our minds. We've even started to put a little money by in the event of it developing.

When we retire, eventually, we want to buy one of

those smart little mobile homes and do some touring: Europe, America ... maybe even Australasia. We could be free agents, stopping and starting and going where we wanted; meeting up with other retired folk and old age pensioners along the way – just befriending them and sharing our treasure – Jesus!

After all, I hadn't really heard the gospel until I was in my mid-twenties. But as it was revealed to me, I fell in love with the simplicity of it all. How Jesus died for me.

I know that there are lots of other people just like that. They may have heard a little about Jesus, but they've never really heard the truth. And I figure that there are lots of older folk who need to be told, too – in a manner that's appropriate for them.

So when people ask me what I'd like to do when I finally stop preaching on the streets, I smile and tell them: 'Buy a camper van.'

If it does work out that way, then I suppose I will finally get round to making that overland trek I'd planned once before. But this time I'll already know where I'm going. And I'll have found what I was looking for.

Afterword

If you've read this far, then I hope you've understood a little about how Jesus can transform your life – even today, even now.

If you have any questions, then please talk them through with someone. Perhaps a Christian friend gave you this book. Talk with a relative or a work colleague who's a Christian, or go along to a local church this Sunday and ask for someone to talk to afterwards.

You can turn to the Bible, too. As God's timeless word, it tells how we have become separated from him through sin – but also points to the way back, through Jesus. Take some time to read and study it for yourself, maybe starting with John's Gospel. Ask God to help you understand it.

Perhaps you think that you're OK because you've never done anything as wicked as I did. Well, that's not what the Bible says. It states that every one of us has fallen short of God's mark. 'For all have sinned and fall short of the glory of God,' says Romans 3:23. That includes you.

Alternatively, maybe your life has taken you to even darker corners than mine – and you think you've gone too far for God to forgive you. As surely as the Bible says all have sinned, it says all can be forgiven. There's a promise which says: 'If we confess our sins, he is faithful and just and will forgive us.' That covers you, too.

You may want to know that forgiveness in your life. I hope so. Perhaps you want to think it all through a bit more first – or maybe you are ready to receive it right now. You can.

Just pray this short prayer, right now:

'Father God, I believe that you have been speaking to me and showing me that I am separated from you by sin. I believe that Jesus Christ, your only Son, was crucified and rose from the dead, taking my punishment so that I may be forgiven. I ask you to forgive all my sins in his name, and ask Jesus to come into my life and take control. I turn my back on all that has passed, and offer my life to you from this day on. I thank you that you are answering my prayer even now, through the power of the Holy Spirit. In Jesus' name, Amen.'

If you've prayed this short prayer: congratulations! Welcome to the family!

Don't keep it to yourself. Tell some Christians that you know. They will want to encourage and help you in the days to come.

For further information about Youth With a Mission in the United Kingdom, please write to:
Youth With a Mission
13 Highfield Oval,
Ambrose Lane,
Harpenden,
Hertfordshire
AL5 4BX
Tel 0582 65481

From Fury to Freedom

by Raul Ries with Lela Gilbert

Brought up by a drunken father and hardened in a rough school, no one could have been surprised when Raul Ries turned street fighter. To his family he was a time-bomb, ready to explode at any moment. To those who fought beside him in Vietnam he was a cold killer.

Then something happened that turned his life upside down. No more restlessness, no more fury, but instead an inner peace and a new found love.

'God took Raul from the pits of hell, from the cocoon of despair, insecurity, fear, hate and self-destruction, into the most wonderful healing—salvation: the healing of his soul and spirit.'

Nicky Cruz

The story of Raul Ries is also told in a feature film, available from Christian World, Manchester.

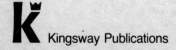

Kingsway Publications

The Father Heart of God

by Floyd McClung

What is God like?

Has he got time for twentieth-century men and women?

Does he really care?

In his work with *Youth with a Mission*, Floyd McClung has met many who suffer from deep emotional hurts and fears.

Time and again it has been the discovery of God as Father—perfect and reliable, unlike any human parent—that has brought healing and liberty.

This book is for you...

...if you find it hard to accept God as a loving father, or
...if you know God's love but would like to share his blessing with others more effectively.

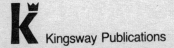

Kingsway Publications